WILLIAM FARNON

A happy Christmas to
the Duns Scotus of
the underprivileged

Bill and Eileen

VAGABOND SCHOLAR

A Venture Into The Privacy
of George Santayana

GEORGE SANTAYANA IN 1950   *Portrait by Lipinsky*

VAGABOND SCHOLAR

A VENTURE
INTO THE PRIVACY
OF GEORGE SANTAYANA

by

BRUNO LIND

Bridgehead Books: New York

1962

FOR JOSEPH BEUTEL
*who first saw this
book and liked it.*

TABLE OF CONTENTS

ACKNOWLEDGMENTS

GRATEFUL ACKNOWLEDGMENT is hereby made to Miss Marg-Riette Montgomery, Mrs. Miriam Ullrich Wagner, Mr. Allan Stehling, and to my father, who read the MS and made many valuable suggestions; also to Mr. Daniel M. Cory who, besides the foregoing, permitted quotation from certain of his letters.

" Blow what winds would, the ancient truth was mine,
And friendship mellowed in the flush of wine,
And heavenly laughter, shaking from its wings
Atoms of light and tears for mortal things."

I. I N T R O D U C T I O N, with CORRESPONDENCE
from October 22, 1950 to February 17, 1951

Vagabond Scholar

I.

"NOTHING," writes George Santayana, "requires a rarer intellectual heroism than willingness to see one's equation written out."

With this in mind, the reader of the present volume is entitled to fair play. No scheme so grandiose as writing an equation for Santayana is here proposed. In another volume, BOHEMIAN OF THE INFINITE, I do frame a partial equation—and even a solution to that equation. The present book is more modest in scope. It is in fact a journey into the private life of the sage, made preparatory to the larger work, as yet unpublished.

Round the work of the most articulate of writers, I told Santayana one afternoon, there is a penumbra. Within such a penumbra lurk nuances. These nuances I hoped to elicit through extended personal talks with him in his "cell" on the Caelius, one of the seven hills of Rome. This, then, is a record of our talks and of our correspondence before and after my visit there just ten years ago.

If classicism were not defunct, I might have entitled this book SAGE ON THE CAELIUS. Unfortunately, the sage himself was sceptical about his own sagacity. "In spite of being so much in sympathy with the sages," he says of himself, "I am well aware of not having been one of them." The most he admits is, "I am an old fogy and almost an ancient philosopher, and I don't count." He does occasionally refer to himself as a "laughing philosopher." But are laughing philosophers to be taken seriously? As I said, there are nuances . . .

Consider this passage from a posthumous essay, THE IDLER AND HIS WORKS. There he tells us, "I have seldom been con-

13

scious of working hard. The things wrote themselves." The "things" in question were some twenty-six volumes of poetry and prose, not to mention numerous fugitive pieces now listed in encyclopedic bibliographies. How many authors could be delivered of such an opus without the consciousness of working hard? Would ambitious young writers of today confess that their "things" wrote themselves?

A lady once offered Santayana a wreath of laurel. He responded:

> *Laurel is a sacred leaf*
> *And forbidden to be worn*
> *Lest Apollo, flushed with scorn,*
> *Shoot the rhymester for a thief.*

Pedants might gather that Santayana was in truth no worker, no poet—much less a sage. Others—of whom I am happy to be one—relish the thought that here, for once, is a philosopher blessed with humor, humanity—and humility.

A sage of antique vintage transported by a miracle into modern times: that is how Santayana has always appeared to me. True, his middle years were spent in the spirit of the middle ages. At that time he lived the life of a medieval *vagans*, travelling freely from cathedral town to cathedral town, from university to university: a typical vagabond scholar. Hence the title of this book.

But late in life, gravitating to the "non-hypocritical Mediterranean world" that he had loved so long, he settled in Rome. His place of sojourn became the Caelian Mount, which overlooks the Colosseum. It was to his cell, as he called it, on the Caelius that in 1950 I addressed my first presumptious letter.

With the letter I enclosed an article written by me about him for the ENGLISH-SPANISH REVIEW. This article dealt briefly with what I was thinking of saying about him at length in BOHEMIAN OF THE INFINITE. I solicited his comment and, if possible, his aid in preparing the study.

He replied promptly. He offered to help in any way feasible. He also concurred with the description I have just given of him, as being a sage or hermit whose way of life—he added—is "like that of the ancient Cynics or Sceptics, with a little Epicureanism to soften it."

When, after further correspondence, I decided to visit him at the clinic of the Blue Sisters, where he was a paying guest, I felt encouraged by something Edmund Wilson had written about Santayana in the NEW YORKER.

"One of the wonderful things about him," Wilson had reported, "was . . . the readiness and grace with which he lived up to a classical rôle: that of the sage . . . who will talk about the purpose and practice of life with anyone who likes to discuss them—as with me, whom he didn't know from Adam—since these are matters which concern us all."

My own reception by Santayana in the spring of 1951 was courteous, as Wilson had led me to expect, but heartier. For this, I surmise, there was a good reason. We were no strangers. I say this though neither of us had ever laid eyes before on the other.

For a score of years reports had reached me about Santayana. The most direct came through my late esteemed friend, Dr. George Rowland Dodson of St. Louis, a former pupil of the philosopher. The two had met at a sidewalk café during the thirties in Paris. In due time, Dr. Dodson related their talks to me. Sporadically, other bits of news drifted to me through his mediation.

Then, as a Whitehead fan at Harvard, I was frequently admonished to read Santayana, which I did. The word, "fan," calls for comment. Actually, though I took numerous courses under Dr. Alfred North Whitehead, I never lost a sense that under him we students were more like fans of the Boston Braves than scholars of philosophy at Harvard. Upstairs, in Emerson Hall, roosted the Positivists. They were not our team! Downstairs, with the men of feeling, foregathered our team, of which Whitehead was the star—a luminary, by the way, of deep humility. This man of feeling would urge us (with great feeling) to read a philosopher who, by his own account, belonged on the other team—if not among the Positivists, at least among those hard-boiled, crystal-clear thinkers of the French Enlightenment, the Rationalists. "Read Santayana," Whitehead would say, and it was not in the tone of Cassandra urging us to read him and weep. Whitehead was a sincere admirer of Santayana. His admiration, I regret, was not so warmly returned.

Casual contacts, however, were not the real foundation on which my familiarity with Santayana was built. In the course of twenty years I managed to read about half his works, some repeatedly. Apparently they left their trace, for when the sage replied to my first letter, he commented, "You seem to know all my books and a good deal about my life, and your proposed final volume with me for a nucleus will be excellent."

We met, then, not as strangers, but as friends from the first. This helped us to leap many hurdles, such as differences of age, nationality, taste, training and the like. These might otherwise have proved insurmountable.

I think I can say without exaggeration that our friendship, which only began in October, 1950, helped brighten the last days of this hermit's life. As for me, having known both Whitehead and Santayana, I feel that I have clasped hands with the Plato and the Aristotle of the twentieth century. No one, I think, could emerge from such acquaintance quite the same.

Now, I should be less than frank, in offering this little collection of letters and talks to the public, were I not to admit at the outset its strict limitation. Many friends must have been closer to Santayana than I. Their memoirs and the correspondence in their possession should see the light of day. Indeed, before a definitive biography can be written, they must. Mr. Bernard Berenson knew Santayana intimately. Are there, in the estate of the lately deceased connoisseur, memoirs about Santayana? Mr. Bertrand Russell has written me that he never had custody of his brother's correspondence with Santayana. Some of it, however, has come to light. Mr. Russell himself could write excellent memoirs on the subject. Mr. Daniel Cory, Santayana's trusted secretary in his declining years and his literary executor, has already published a collection of letters, and has written the definitive account of the sage's last illness. A good deal of Santayana's early correspondence has already been published, notably his student letters to William James, in Ralph Barton Perry's THE THOUGHT AND CHARACTER OF WILLIAM JAMES. William Lyon Phelps has published some of Santayana's badinage in AUTOBIOGRAPHY WITH LETTERS. Finally, there are the letters to Logan Pearsall Smith in UNFORGOTTEN YEARS. Other miscellaneous correspondence is listed in a bibliographical index to THE PHILOSOPHY OF GEORGE SANTAYANA, edited by Paul A. Schilpp. But of all the correspondence which I have seen to date, I believe Santayana's letters to me are unique.

They are unique for their verve, their warmth, their youthfulness and their coherence of expression—from a man nearing his ninetieth year! They are unique for their lack of affectation and for the absence of that oracular tone so often deadly to the relations of elders with their juniors. (After all, the sage was born in 1863, I in 1909!) They are unique for the little story they tell, complete in itself, about Santayana the man. The letters are remarkable, moreover, for their intimacy and frankness.

Never, in questioning him, did I pull my punches, so to speak. Nor did he. Once I asked, rather impertinently, whether his friend, Lord Francis Russell, had ever killed a man. I had dreamt up a theory after reading VERA, a novel written by Russell's exasperated ex-wife. I got my answer from Santayana, straightforward and jolly: No! Finally, these letters are unique for their style. One or two are perfect little essays in themselves. Others, being answers to a hodge-podge of queries from me, are not so unified. They are never dull.

In spots, which I have indicated, the infirmities of age intervened. Here and there an obvious word or syllable would be left out. The letters, however, are generally strong in thought and sparkling in style—no small feat for an octogenarian. The script, as the reader can see, remained bold and firm almost to the end. The last note, written in pencil, wavers. "My eyes," he explained, "are getting weak and uncertain, so that both reading and writing are difficult." In view of the circumstances I know of few braver words.

The facts were these. At the time that I first met him, Santayana already suffered from a cataract in one eye and weakness in the other. This left him almost totally blind. He was also partially deaf. He nursed a chronic bronchial catarrh. Despite these handicaps, he continued his correspondence, which was wide, and his work, which was formidable. After his last book, DOMINATIONS AND POWERS, had appeared in print he planned to relax. Nevertheless, he was making investigations for a study on Alexander the Great. Then Scribners persuaded him to undertake a revised edition of THE LIFE OF REASON— five volumes!

"We must nerve ourselves up to condense whole pages and chapters," he wrote me at this time.

Thereafter, he fell backwards on the steps of the Spanish consulate, contracted pneumonia, staged an amazing recovery, and only succumbed in the end to cancer of the stomach, whose extreme stages, fortunately, lasted only a few days.

During these final weeks he translated from the Italian Lorenzo de' Medici's poem, AMBRA. The stamina of this man, who habitually claimed that he was "indolent," "soft," and "luxurious" will leave its imprint on my mind forever. If ever a man had grit it was Santayana. He was an intellectual hero.

In presenting the sage's letters, then, I do so happy in the friendship they reveal, and confident that they will be of unusual interest to artists, philosophers, and intellectuals the world over.

In offering my own dialogues with him, which extended over a period of seventeen days, I feel on the other hand a certain diffidence.

I am not a reporter. These conversations are not stenographic. They were written down at my hotel immediately after our talks, which lasted from one to three hours. Some notes were used. On doubtful points I raised questions the next day. But for the most part I had to rely on my memory. I made no great attempt to reproduce the style of Santayana's conversation, except for a striking phrase here and there. (As others have observed, it was not so rich in subtle insinuation as his writing.) I was concerned chiefly with his thought. This I think I reproduced accurately.

At the time I recorded these talks, though I had a vague notion they might be published, my chief concern was to jot down for myself as much *background* for BOHEMIAN OF THE INFINITE as I could gather. After all, Santayana's style can be savoured from reading of his numerous poems and essays. His thought, too, is expressed in the collected works as well as any sage ever expressed it. What I went to Rome to obtain were rather those nuances cast over an author's work by personal acquaintance, plus any data that might have been omitted from PERSONS AND PLACES—his autobiography—should such details seem to have importance.

This much I assert without apology. I obtained what I was looking for in Rome—and more. I learned the connection between Santayana's family life and the plot of THE LAST PURITAN. I guessed and verified the true identity of Lord Jim in that novel —something Santayana had cautioned William Lyon Phelps not to reveal to the public long years before. I learned Santayana's peculiar attitude toward women. He discussed his writing income frankly with me, which in view of mistakes spread about it by some of his critics deserves an airing. He identified two individuals who appear only as *A* and *B* in PERSONS AND PLACES— as well as another, known there only as Mme. Blanc Blanc. For me this was ample.

It would be a mistake, however, for scholars to treat these talks as source-material in the same sense as the correspondence. The dialogues should be regarded rather as background: suggestive hints useful for penetrating beneath the surface of Santayana's writing—but nothing more.

It is of course not true, as Santayana himself points out in SOLILOQUIES IN ENGLAND, that contemporaries understand a man less well than does posterity. Quite the contrary. A contemporary knows—if anyone knows—how to read between the lines.

And of course, in the literary world, anything connected with Santayana is big game territory. Fortunately, it will never be all staked off as the private domain of fusty academicians.

Inevitably, our trans-Atlantic relationship struck a few snags. One arose from the detail that I write under the name of my grandparents: the only name by which Santayana ever knew me. How did this happen?

It began as an accident. I had heard that he was feeble and liable to lose the thread of a conversation. (In my talks with him we discussed this very point. The reader must judge for himself how feeble or how incoherent the sage had actually grown.) The point is, I couldn't know the situation in advance. He was already in possession of my article, signed Bruno Lind. Would it confuse the old man or change our relationship, I wondered, if suddenly I appeared under a new name?

A more powerful consideration influenced me, however, to let well enough alone. My real name is Germanic. I had reason to believe, after reading EGOTISM IN GERMAN PHILOSOPHY, as well as remarks of Santayana elsewhere, that he was prejudiced against Germans. On closer acquaintance I found this to be false, but how could I know this in advance? I decided to go, then, as Lind—a name which sounds (and is) Swedish, so that Santayana need not feel constrained when airing his views to me on any subject. Later, I asked myself: Ought I not write him the truth, now that we are friends? Always I returned to the same thought: A rose by another name smells just as sweet—or sour.

A final difficulty ought not be glossed over. Why, after recording these talks, did I not send them all to Santayana to be checked? In certain cases, which I thought of supreme importance, I did. Here, however, I felt that the main responsibility was mine. I had noticed in our talks little slips which indicated lapses of memory. They were minor lapses, but slips nonetheless. Speaking of Robert Lowell, for instance, Santayana said he had not been familiar with a word used by Lowell in a poem, namely:

"taproot." He had had to look it up in a dictionary! Yet I have since found the word used by him in a recent work. (MY HOST THE WORLD, page 144.) When shaving, he confessed, he had to do things always in the same order. Otherwise he was no longer sure whether he had shaved or not! These and other little slips suggested an unpleasant possibility.

If I sent the dialogues to Santayana in their entirety, besides the bother to him, what if he didn't recall them? The whole situation might prove embarrassing and nothing would be gained.

Something like this actually occurred when I sent him the Preface to BOHEMIAN OF THE INFINITE. "In my first reading," he commented, "I thought perhaps you repeated your classification too much, and that 'intellectuals' was vague. But I felt this less on the second reading; also missed altogether a quotation that I meant to ask you to leave out, although I did not understand it." The quotation in point was, I presume, the following: " 'Of course,' Santayana once said to me, 'some day someone will look up all the sources and print everything about me—they always do; but it won't be important.' " Now, whether the sage remembered it or not, that is what he said, stated as accurately as I could recall it immediately after the event—as long, that is, as it took me to walk down from Caelius, past the Colosseum, up the *Via Del Corso,* and into the *Albergo d'Inghilterra* where I was staying. But of this I have perhaps said enough. The value of the dialogues will depend, in any event, on the light they throw on known works of Santayana.

The conversationalist and correspondent here depicted is best known as a philosopher. I must devote a word to the manner in which I approached him. I could not address him as a professional philosopher. I am no such thing. I am, as I said, only a fan—or as the Spaniards put it, *un aficionado.* I like philosophy as I like bullfights. I have written no books of philosophy. I expect—barring accidents!—to fight no bulls. The professional will therefore look here in vain for anything professionally remarkable. He will perhaps find nothing he has not read in Santayana before. My own point of view, if one must use jaw-breaking expressions, has been psycho-sociological: but again in no professional sense. I was intrigued as a layman with the relationship between Santayana, the man, and modern society.

Such an interest is not wholly eccentric. The last portion of PERSONS AND PLACES, which I was permitted to read in Rome in the typescript, discloses that Santayana's professional career was not his life. He abandoned professorial duties as soon as he could. A hint dropped in the chapter on "Liberation" in THE REALM OF SPIRIT has also been my guide. "Perhaps," Santayana writes there, " a surer and more positive idea of liberation may be drawn from observing what spiritual men are than by discussing what they say." For the present I shall pursue this topic no further.

To return to the correspondence.* I have divided it into two parts: as it fell before and after my visit to Santayana in Rome. The first part involves only three letters.

Below, Santayana deals with certain questions posed in my initial letter to him. This had included the article in the ENGLISH-SPANISH REVIEW. I had dealt in that article with a fusion and confusion of tongues in Texas, a blend of Spanish and English, known as *Pachuco*. For the rest, my letter had outlined the proposed volume about him. It was to be one of a series on writers who had led Bohemian lives. His volume was to be the last of that series. I had suggested his place there by the following paragraph:

"What began as an individual problem with Poe: the intellectual crying in the wilderness—alone; what continued as a group-problem with the Bohemians: intellectuals pitted against the Philistines, ends in our time with a philosophical problem for all of society: the nature and claims of the spiritual life as they touch the lives of everyone. You have posed the problem clearly. You have blazed new trails out of the wilderness. That, in my series, is your prime importance in the history of Bohemianism."

Santayana's answer is transcribed below. The Howgate referred to by him is the author of a biography written in 1936.
*Original MS now in the Houghton Library, Harvard University.

The reference to Russell arose out of a mistake I had made in the article. I had called him the Earl *of* Russell instead of simply Earl Russell.

Via Santo Stefano Rotondo, 6,
Rome, October 22, 1950

Dear Mr. Lind:

You have written an astonishingly penetrating sketch of me and my philosophy, the most sympathetic I have yet seen. You seem to know all my books and a good deal about my life, and your proposed final volume with me for a nucleus will be excellent. Naturally where you have no first-hand account to go on you let your sympathetic imagination fill in the picture, as people must writing biographies, even autobiographies. But you may get further facts and hints from other studies of my works which have appeared. Howgate is accurate about facts up to the date of his book, which I had read in proof, but he has not, to my knowledge, kept up with the rest; and he is fair about style, etc., but not very intelligent *in excelsis*. I notice in your article one or two small slips in details. I was born on Dec. 16, 1863, not 4; and my friend's title was Earl Russell, not of, since this is also his family surname; and he did not remain always as expansive and trustful a friend as he was in the first years. This is described in the third part of "Persons and Places," not yet published. You also overemphasise a little my attachment to Spain. It is largely theoretical. It was Greece and England—one also theoretical and the other fragmentary—that were in my mind when I wrote the "Life of Reason."

I have just received a thick volume entitled "Le Pensée de George Santayana en Amerique" by Jacques Duron, Librarie Nizet, Paris. A second volume seems to be intended, I suppose on my "Pensée en Europe." This would be a very good pacemaker for you, when you come to your final volume. Duron is a *trained* philosopher, employed in the Ministry of Instruction, not now a teacher; and he has tact and discretion on personal matters. It is all arranged systematically, in chronological order, and would be easy to consult on particular points.

Now as to Bohemia, I think we should distinguish accidental bohemians, such because they are loose in Paris with little
money and no roots or family friends, and bohemians in the
sense of free souls, taking life at first hand and defying conventions of every kind. I don't think it is so much intelligence as art
that moves them, and they need not be poor. For instance, there
is Sir Osbert Sitwell, with his brother and Dr. Sister. If you look
at the second paragraph of the introductory part of his "Noble
Essences" you will find a description of the social-political world,
not all bourgeois in an economic sense (it includes Eton, for instance) but inveighs chiefly against dullness. It represents the
intellectuals (he says rather "artists") as the only possible saviours
of the world.

Now my bohemianism, if any, is more like that of the ancient
Cynics or Sceptics, with a little Epicureanism to soften it; for I
do not despise convention, even in painting or poetry; I like it
when, as in Racine, (sic) for I love perfection, which has to be
definite and exclusive of everything else. But as you say perfection of one sort is to be transcended, not by lapsing into imper-
fection in that art, but by seeing the equal perfection possible
in an entirely different art, when it is the natural realisation of an
autonomous impulse in a man, or a class, or a nation. Heresies
within a system are simply wrong-headed, but sects, like those in
ancient philosophy, are alternative forms of virtue. I am not at
all a bohemian, then, in being a rebel to academic philosophy or
art or to polite society—there is where my friends the Russells
have come to grief—but in keeping my spirit free to accept, if
circumstances permit or impose it, some other type of polite
society or academic art. The mind is gregarious, more than the
body, but it must flock with its own kind of its own accord, to
the immense enhancement of its wealth and glory. So I should
say to your two nationalities or languages at San Antonio: Don't
fuse them; keep them pure each for its own occasions. Didn't
the Athenian tragedians write their dialogues in Attic and their
choruses in Doric? And didn't Charles V say Latin was best for
addressing God, Spanish for men, Italian for diplomats, French

for women, and German—*for his horse*: but I should have preferred to say for Protestant Hymns and the pastorales of Walter von der Vogelweide.

Yours sincerely,
G. Santayana

Overjoyed with the foregoing charming letter, I made a series of errors. I answered with a six-page letter (single-spaced!), at a time when Santayana must have been deep in the proof-reading of DOMINATIONS AND POWERS. Not only that, I incorporated in my omnibus every stray question I could think of —the kind that can be answered in a moment during a personal interview but which calls for all sorts of tiresome qualification when written out. I sensed this more or less vaguely, and suggested I might have to come to Rome; but since, at the moment, I was working on a book about Baudelaire, and only thought of reaching Santayana's volume some years later, all this remained in a state of flux. Meanwhile, I supposed, I might ply Santayana with questions. One question must have seemed entirely too personal to him on such short acquaintance. I had said:

"If one were writing a novel about you (and my own belief is that biography should read like a novel) the plot would work up to, and down from, certain dramatic crises, with some periods in between which you quaintly dub 'somnambulism'...If you care to indicate important turning-points for me—particularly for the missing Part III of your autobiography, I should be deeply grateful.

"What concerns me about this, aside from the human drama," I continued, "is the connection with your philosophy. An emotional crisis can be a *test* of a philosophy, or its *origin*—sometimes both."

In another question, I had tried to get him to expand his thought, expressed in THE MIDDLE SPAN, on the connection between religion and nationality.

A passage in the same volume alludes to Harvard "social

distinctions" which rested, he said, neither on wealth, breeding nor achievement. "These," I wrote, "are mysterious distinctions. Would you like to enlarge on this?"

That, despite such fumbling on my part, Santayana could write so temperate and helpful a letter as follows, showed me that his chivalrous nature—which he once named Van Tender— underlay his sterner nature—nicknamed Mac Stout—; but I was warned by the letter's tone not to tax him unduly. I had suggested, for example, that if I came to Rome I might bring along a wire recorder, into which he might read some of his sonnets. His brusque refusal convinced me that a trans-Atlantic correspondence without personal contact might lead to misunderstandings. I determined shortly hereafter to go to Rome.

Via Santo Stefano Rotondo, 6,
Rome, Nov. 25, 1950

Dear Mr. Lind:

Your letter is too long and miscellaneous to be answered in the time I have at my disposal at present; and I will warn you that I have nothing to say on the guesses that might be made as to crises or conflicts in my inner life. The matter of religion, and of relations to persons and places, especially nationalities, has been treated in PERSONS AND PLACES as fully as I am able or care to discuss it. As to the third part (it is all one book) the first and last chapters have appeared in THE ATLANTIC under the titles A CHANGE OF HEART and MINE HOST, THE WORLD, and are those that most concern your questions, together with a third chapter of Part III, FAREWELL TO ENGLAND (after the first war). This was more of a conflict and a wrench than my farewell to America, which only fulfilled a lifelong intention. But if you come to Rome and find me alive, you may *read* Part Third if you like while you are here in a typed copy. Beside those chapters just mentioned the others are: KING'S COLLEGE, CAMBRIDGE, TRAVELS, ON THE SOUTH DOWNS (regarding Russell's life with his 2nd & 3d wives) OXFORD FRIENDS, & OLD AGE IN ITALY.

One point you raise that is impersonal—and I shall never lend myself to manufacturing mementoes, by reading sonnets to a machine, or anything of that kind,—regards Harvard College, memories of which in such matters always interest me. The social distinctions there were not official: they touched only the gay part of the undergraduate world and the clubs. If you belonged to a club you know what I mean. From the Porcellian down there was a marked, though variable, hierarchy and I learned how much such divisions could add to the pleasure of life, inherent to each, without any ill-feeling between the various groups. I understand that this social arrangement has outlived and now overshadows the institution of Houses which was well meant by President Lowell but artificial. Things should grow by what in my new book I call the Generative Order of Nature.

Duron will give you a good technical synopsis of my books. I am glad you have ordered the book.

Yours sincerely,
G. Santayana

For me, between the foregoing epistle and the next, a hectic time intervened. Having determined now to fly to Rome, I was deep in governmental red-tape from which, till the very last moment, I doubted if I should ever be extricated. I was also trying to read everything of Santayana's before I saw him. I kept him informed by short bulletins, which I excerpt below:

Feb. 11, 1951

Dear Mr. Santayana:

If it is not too great an inconvenience to you, I shall start my Unholy Year pilgrimage next month. That is to say, *if* certain final hurdles can be leaped—leave to absent myself from the United States being one. (I am in the reserve.) . . . Let me say that I have no notion of monopolizing your time. If you can spare an hour or two now and then, I'll be happy ... If, without *any* extra trouble, you could mention one or two reasonable hotels or pensions within walking distance of your place, I should appreciate it no end . . . Enclosed please find a copy of an item I should like your permission to quote . . . As you are so fond of saying, dialectical necessity takes small note of material events. In many ways my visit at this time will be premature. I resemble a boa-constrictor who has just swallowed all your works. What I really need is to lie in the sun and let all the mass digest . . . Meanwhile, I hope to bask in the winter sunshine of your personality, and perhaps bring you one or two kind greetings from the States.

Santayana's gracious reply follows:

Via Santo Stefano Rotondo, 6,
Rome, Feb. 17, 1951

Dear Mr. Lind:

Your endurance in devouring all my works and desire to digest them make a great bond. I am sorry that living in a hospital I cannot ask you to come and stay with me or even invite you to any meal, as I have mine on a tray in my cell. Moreover, there are no hotels in this part of town, the extreme South; but busses and a "circular" line of trams, running both ways, can bring you from town to the *Colosseo*, from which a broad shady street leads gently up hill to the *Navicella*, a marble Roman fountain (reproduced) on reaching which, by turning sharply to your left you will see a paved lane, with the sign *"Via de Santo Stefano"* on the left wall; and opposite the round brick church of that name, next beyond which, through an open archway in the ruins of an aqueduct, you will find the respectable entrance to the grounds of this establishment with the chief entrance in a porch at the end of the avenue. My leisure hours are the whole afternoon from 2 to 7. Visitors sometimes come but you could regard them as intruders and stay them out.

As to lodgings, if you want to profit by your short stay

and see as much local colour as possible, I should suggest the old *Hôtel d'Angleterre* or *d'Inghilterra* in the very middle of the town (*Via Bocca di Leone*) where you can get a room and breakfast without other meals. The numerous restaurants are crowded and good; you can easily pick up the necessary Italian, and learn what category and what dishes suit you best. My favourites for every day, when I lived in the town, were the *Roma*, the *San Carlo*, and the *Fagiano*. You should have a guide book and a map to consult until you learn the ropes.

It is all right about the quotation from my letter. The "German—to my horse" is a bit rough, but it was probably Flemish that he (Charles V) meant and in any case I have softened the insult to (the) German language.

Yours sincerely,
G. Santayana

Mirabile dictu, my plans for departure were shortly completed. I notified Santayana of my proposed schedule in the letter below.

March 2, 1951

Dear Mr. Santayana:

One by one the hurdles I've had to leap in order to make my trip are being cleared. On the assumption, then, that my rabbit's foot is in good working order, I thought you might like to know my tentative schedule. I shall leave New York by plane Monday, the twelfth. Next afternoon I shall be in Madrid. I plan to stop over there a day, and, if the number hasn't been changed, if the house is still standing, and if the Spanish authorities let me, photograph your birth-place. But never fear: I'm not one of those horrible journalists with a flash-bulb, and I'm not "manufacturing mementoes." Actually, I just thought this might be a chance to see some of Madrid that Franco might otherwise not want me to see. On Wednesday, the fourteenth, I leave Madrid and at 4:55 PM I should be in Rome. I shall check in at the *Hôtel d'Angleterre*, as you suggested, and perhaps, if it is not too late, drop in to greet you. If the plane is late, or for some other unforeseen reason the hour is too advanced, I shall wait until the next day.

All this, of course, is still subject to contingencies. As they say in the Army, I'm sweating out my passport, and haven't heard from the Spanish Consul-general about a visa, which may be long-drawn-out and require 572½ photographs of myself, all identical. If any drastic changes take place, however, I shall notify you; and I suppose mass will be said at St. Peter's whether I arrive on time or not.

Very sincerely yours,
Bruno Lind

Civilian and military gears—both well sanded!—ground out their appointed revolutions. Beneath the plane the diverse land-scapes of Texas, the Atlantic coastal states, then Newfoundland rolled swiftly by.

While we refueled in Gander, an American Army sergeant stationed there informed me that the Yankees were robbing the Newfoundlanders of all their women. His wife was a case in point!

Approaching the Azores, where the landing-strip borders high cliffs along the sea, I remembered Ginette Neveu, the talented young French violinist, killed there in a crash shortly before. In Lisbon I nearly missed the plane while helping an American lady change some money. In Madrid, hard by the church of San Isidro, I was reminded that once again I was in the Mediterranean world. A school-boy, his books tucked under his arm, was pissing freely by the curb, oblivious of passers-by and they of him...

A short hop over Corsica, and the Eternal City rose into view. That part of my mission described in my letter had been accomplished. What follows was written within twenty-four hours after the event. The "interludes"—accounts of days when I did not visit Santayana—were written one month later.

II. CONVERSATIONS, March 16-27, 1951

W HETHER, on leaving the *Albergo d'Inghilterra*, you turn to the left or to the right, if you turn respectively left or right again at the nearest corner, you will reach the *Via Del Corso* in a matter of minutes. This I did, on March 16, 1951, bound for the Convent of Blue Nuns at whose clinic Santayana was staying. My first goal was the Colosseum.

The day was clear, the air brisk. This was the eve of Holy Week but throngs along the *Corso* were gay. Reaching the *Via Dei Fori Imperiali*, I found myself on an avenue lined with daffodils, as far as the eye could see. Passing a ruined basilica, I recognized on its walls four maps depicting the growth of the Roman Empire. I had seen them in 1927 as a youth. Mussolini had placed them there—a hint to latter-day *"Romani."* Hewn from stone, the maps lingered on intact. Only *Mare Nostrum*, originally painted blue, shown blue no longer. Gray and faded now, the Mediterranean was comparable to *Il Duce's* comic-opera empire itself, already vanished. Meanwhile, surviving *"Romani"* strolled gaily back and forth—oblivious, if not ignorant, of so much tarnished splendor.

"A broad shady street," Santayana had written me, "leads gently (*from the Colosseum*) up hill to the *Navicella*, a marble Roman fountain (reproduced)." It was indeed so: the *Via Claudia*. "By turning sharply to your left," Santayana had continued, "you will see a paved lane, with the sign *"Via de Santo Stefano"* on the left wall; and opposite the round brick church of that name, next beyond which, through an open archway in the ruins of an aqueduct, you will find the respectable entrance to the grounds of this establishment."

All this I found—save the entrance aforementioned. Not noticing the number 6 on the wall, I passed some distance beyond. Perplexed, I spoke to some nuns on the street, in English. They did not understand. At my mention of *"il professore"*, however, a man standing nearby exclaimed, *"Ah, la clinica!"* and directed me to it.

31

As I rang the first doorbell I saw, a door in the other wing of the clinic opened. A maid beckoned. I entered a lobby over which presided, at the far end, a large figure of the Virgin: *Maria Consolatrix Afflictorum.* Opening a heavy oak door to the left of the figure, I found myself in a curving hall. A maid pointed to the right-hand door at the far end of the hall. With heart beating faster than usual I knocked.

"You are two days late," said Santayana, after formal salutations. I explained that, according to the dates I had written him, I was actually only one day late. His question suggested that he had been looking forward to my visit. I hoped so.

Santayana had risen from a chaise-longue placed in front of a high window—one of two windows in what could only metaphorically be called a "cell." He offered me a small armchair. He seated himself at the foot of his chaise-longue. I protested that he would be uncomfortable.

"I always sit here," he explained, "when people come. You see, I'm nearly blind and partly deaf. I can see you at this moment moving in the light, but I shouldn't recognize you tomorrow. Oh, now I see you wear glasses and have dark eye-brows."

While he spoke, I noticed the British accent. His eyes, quite large, had a wide-open look, as if he were trying to see as much as possible. The slight mark on his nose from small-pox, mentioned in PERSONS AND PLACES, was visible, as well as a slight discoloration on the right cheek, betraying the work of time.

Contrary to Edmund Wilson's report, however, Santayana did not strike me as sallow or small. He was not tall—possibly five feet six—but his weight, not excessive or unpleasing, gave him a substantial appearance. His manner was cautiously cordial from the outset. Meanwhile, in answer to my question, "How can you read? I see your room is full of books," he continued his clinical report.

"Oh, I read a great deal. But this eye," (he indicated the right one) "has a cataract, and the other was never much good.

It's no use operating, the doctor says, at my age. In fact, when you grow old one thing gives, then another. I'm losing my teeth. I wanted them pulled, but they told me not to have it done. They fall out by themselves, one by one. It's not painful that way. The other day I lost two. I just thought they were some bones in the food."

(The second right lateral upper incisor, I noticed, was long and loose. In general, however, the sage did not appear decrepit, as the details above might suggest.)

THE KID by Conrad Aiken was lying on the desk, amid a pile of other books.

"When I was getting ready to come," I explained, "I tried to think of something to bring you. I have THE KID by Aiken, but I thought you wouldn't be interested in that sort of thing."

"Oh, he was a friend," Santayana replied, "as you may remember from Part II of PERSONS AND PLACES. (It has a different name but it's all one book.) He was the leading light of my second poetry circle. Really, it was a kind of seminar. All we read was Shelley. We'd take turns reading aloud, he and I."

I mentioned wanting to bring a volume of Robinson Jeffers, but finding his work scarce and out of print, could not. Santayana did not know of him. He apologized for the litter of books, saying he had many more stored away in the next room. I gathered that a huge cloth screen opposite one window (his was a corner room) hid a tub or wash-stand—not books.

Meanwhile, in wistful contrast to his own dim vision, Santayana called my attention to one window. "I have a view," he said. The gesture, mentioned in PERSONS AND PLACES, was Bostonian.

I rose and looked. He pointed out a distant *campanile* and the ancient Roman walls.

"They curve over there," he said, "so that we are included. They aren't good walls. They were built in the late Empire, I believe."

Sitting down again, he shot me an inquiring look.

"I stopped two days in Madrid," I volunteered.

"Oh," he exclaimed happily, "did you get a picture of the house?" (I had written that I intended to photograph his birthplace.)

"Yes," I replied, "and I wanted to go to Avila, but a landslide covered part of the railroad, and it was impossible. I also photographed a church near your house which I thought was *San Marcos*. It turned out, when I inquired around, that it was *Monserrat*. I finally found *San Marcos* and took a picture. I'll have it developed so that you can tell me if it's the right one."

"I was only back there once," said Santayana. "It's over ten years since I was in Spain and over thirty since I was in the states ... The house had three storeys." He explained that in Spain the first storey isn't counted.

"Then," I decided, "the house I photographed has been torn down or added to."

"That could be," he replied. "They often go on adding storey to storey."

Without thinking, I remarked that I had been in Madrid during Holy Week.

"Oh, no!" he objected. "Next week is Holy Week."

"Well," I said, "there was a great deal of preparation. Everyone in the churches I visited seemed in mourning."

"That's Spain," Santayana declared. "They're bringing all that back there now. It's very impressive to see those processions going by in dead silence."

The mayor of Madrid, I remembered, had posted a decree forbidding all traffic to move along certain streets during Holy Week.

"In Spain," Santayana explained, "when they lose someone, it's not unusual for them to go into mourning for life. Actually, it makes things simpler. So many of them belong to what is now called the *bourgeois* class."

This particular shaft at what I had supposed was largely a theocratic state caught me off stride. I could only flounder around and come out lamely with the remark: "They seem to make a cult of death. Here in Rome I was greeted with just the opposite. Everyone seems in love with life. Next to my hotel, last night, some kind of men's club was singing away..."

"Oh, yes. They don't observe Holy Week in Rome as they do in Spain. Good Friday is a feast-day here. They often celebrate it twice."

"I was wondering," I mused, "where I might hear some good music at this time. I had thought of St. John of the Lateran."

"That's as good as any. The voices won't be anything special —I mean the soloists."

"I thought they had a choir."

"They do. It's a good one. But the quartets won't be sung by professionals."

"Well, in any case, the contrast is striking. In Rome, life; in Spain, death."

"Yes, they're bringing all that back. And then, Spanish funerals are so pompous."

"I never cared for them," Santayana went on. "They're just like banquets in honor of somebody. You know in advance what will be said. Ordinarily no new anecdotes are told."

"Funerals," I agreed, "are barbarous."

At this juncture Santayana's poor hearing played him false. "Yes," he said, "I suppose I should go to the barber."

Then, apparently sensing that he had misunderstood, he quickly added, "I shouldn't know anyone in Madrid. I've out-lived all my friends."

"Not all—at least in the States," I argued. "John Dewey was just honored at a banquet on his ninetieth birthday. But he insisted there should be no fuss. He had been canonised, he said, at seventy, and didn't want to go through all that again."

"Seventy is a nice age," Santayana assented, overlooking the irony of my including Dewey among his friends. Then, without transition (disconcerting, no doubt, to those who have not read him) he continued: "I suppose one is influenced without know-ing it." (He was referring, obviously, to Dewey's pragmatic school.) "When I was young I was influenced by Percy."

"Percy?" I asked blankly.*

"Don't you know him, the pragmatist? Well, nobody could hire him. He was a drunkard. But when he was sober! I heard some of his lectures. I remember particularly an illustration he used—a thermometer. It's a dynamic symbol—anything telling you quantity. That, of course, fits in with my system. I distinquish between the dynamic side of nature and all the imaginative or symbolic side, which is just ideas."

"What do you think of the vogue of semantics?" I asked.

"I don't know about it."

"It's a study of the symbolic process. I believe you anticipated the movement. You would like a book by Langer called PHILOSOPHY IN A NEW KEY. She makes a study of art and religion."

"Oh!"—disappointedly—"it's a woman!"

"Yes. Her husband is also a history teacher at Harvard. You'd be surprised at the number of people working in this field. Then, have you seen Northrop's MEETING OF EAST AND WEST?"

"No, I haven't. I did correspond with Professor Moore at Honolulu University. They're getting out a quarterly on that. You'll see a gray book over there on the table, about Tibet. It's very good."

For the first time, I took out a notebook. I had tried to respect Santayana's dislike for "apparatus," and intended transcribing the conversations from memory later.

"I don't know if you care for that sort of thing," said Santayana. The book was SEGRETO TIBET by Fosco Maraini. Santayana turned the volume over. It showed a photograph of a Tibetan idol—a woman, with pigs' heads for breasts.

"It's rather shocking," he said, "but Maraini explains it in a way that's unusual. They don't worship monsters. Those are gods, but made up so that they frighten away devils. The Tibetan religion, you know, is a mixture. It has Buddhist elements—

*Charles Peirce. I had never heard the name pronounced in this manner.

they're a very old, special Buddhist sect. Then there's the
Chinese influence. You don't often find a good book on that:
the Hindu element especially. When the Hindus write about
their religion in English I always get the impression they're
trying to please the Anglo-Saxons."

Here Santayana indulged in a hearty laugh. By now, in fact,
his earlier reticence had worn off. His face lighted up. Peals of
laughter followed one another—sometimes for no obvious cause
except, as I hoped, that he felt at home in my company. I, in
turn, gesticulated freely in traditional Latin fashion—a thing
which seemed to please him.

"How I wish you knew the Southwest," I exclaimed. "There
they are struggling with the same problem—a mixture of cultures."

"It can't be imposed," Santayana declared. "Something of
mine is coming out in that Honolulu magazine—just a letter
telling them I was interested in the venture. Then, I think, I
wrote you along the same line. It's taken up also in DOMINATIONS
AND POWERS.

"Will that be out soon?" I asked.

"This month. You know, they put out an edition for the
reviewers a month ahead. I'm supposed to receive at least three
copies. They may arrive while you're here."

"I'm astonished at your productivity. When did you actually finish it?"

"Oh, it's an early work. Cory helped me get it out. Cory's
my secretary. He was very helpful. Of course I write my own
letters. I was dissatisfied with REASON IN SOCIETY. Not REASON
IN RELIGION!—I stand by that. But you see, when Plato and
Aristotle wrote about forms of government and the good society,
they had one people in mind. I can't prescribe in that way. I'm
not a moralist. I'm not God, or thinking of taking his place!
(This with some heat.) If you ask what is the right form of
government you have to give me something to work with. The
good is relative to a particular being . . . I should like to do something historical on the subject, but it would take a lot of study.
I can't do it, but it's something you might do."

"What is the general plan?"

"I wanted to analyze several attempts to impose a culture. There was Alexander, for example. He tried to make his Macedonians into Persians. When he received tribute from the Persians he dressed like them. He set up satrapies. But there was always a faction against him. Once the Macedonians revolted, but he put the revolt down with a speech. (He was a great orator.) 'We are all brothers,' he said. Then when he died you have Macedonians as Oriental despots, but they spoke Greek! And it was the Greek influence you see in Egyptian religion—Plato, Plotinus. There's not much Egyptian there."

"Then there's Byzantium. Of course it lasted a thousand years, but was it a success? Justinian wanted to succeed where the West failed, and actually the Eastern empire outlived the West. But it wasn't Roman; it was Greek."

"And the Balkans," I remarked, "have never yet been united."

"Still, the Greek language lasted," said Santayana. "Of course, so has the Latin—more so, probably, than the Greek."

"Plato, they say, could read a modern newspaper."

"But he wouldn't understand it!" Santayana laughed.

He went on to explain how modern Greek poets, using rhyme, make every rhyme *e*, because the vowels, since Plato's time, have changed. Santayana recalled that he owed this bit of knowledge to a visiting speaker at the Boston Latin School during his youth.

I asked, "But what other empire were you thinking of studying?"

"Well, the Church. It has Oriental elements—one is near-east, Jewish. That's the practical side: worship of the natural order."

"You call it 'prudential religion.' "

"Yes. You are good and you behave yourself and God rewards you. He makes you a success."

(Here Santayana laughed heartily.)

"But of course that's not all." He tapped the book on Tibet. "There's this: much more religious, actually, and an entirely different type of religious life."

"Do you feel that the Church succeeded in mixing the two elements?"

"Well, it has developed its own tradition about it—but I feel there's a great deal of illusion on the subject. There are so many orders with different ideals. At first they were all Bene-dictines. They were devoted to learning and doing the ritual correctly. Then came the Franciscans, the Jesuits, the Domini-cans. The Little Company of Mary here is fairly new. A niece of the founder still lives here."

Santayana mentioned various chapters scattered over the world: in Ireland, the United States, even Australia.

"They are nursing nuns?"

"They are nuns first," answered Santayana, "then nurses. The first year is devoted entirely to religion. They say that makes them better nurses in the end." Reverting to the original subject, he continued: "The Protestants, of course, took up the com-mercial side."

Here, in a heated digression, he burst out, "Another thing I wish somebody would write is a refutation of the entire English school, beginning with Locke!"

Having been invited to write a book of history, I hesitated to follow this new lead. After all, I wasn't a philosopher. Santay-ana quickly returned to the preceding topic.

"This idea of success if God is on your side is commercial. It's the Bostonian, the American idea. When the Book-of-the-Month club took up my LAST PURITAN, my nephew in Boston said, 'You ought to write another; it'll make you a lot of money!'"

Santayana laughed at this till tears came to his eyes.

"You cheat and you steal," he went on, "but you must do it honestly."

"Honesty," I parodied, "is the best *policy*."

"If the Bible says anything to the contrary," Santayana laughed, "you revise the Bible. The Bible is wrong."

"That is in line with what I wrote you," I said, "about different philosophies growing out of social classes. Do you think there's anything to it?"

"Yes," he said, "except that you have your Puritan strain. They combined religion and commerce. You must never be idle. You must be strictly honest. You must love your work—in spite of what the Bible says about work. That took the fun out of the cheating and stealing!"

(More laughter. I made a mental note of the permutations and combinations possible among class-attitudes. I saw also that some of these hybrids would be unstable and disappear. Such disintegration seems actually to have occurred in Puritanism.)

"I was writing a man in London," said Santayana, "about a Spanish translation of THE IDEA OF CHRIST." Santayana was evidently dwelling on the subject of royalties. "I believe they got the edition out in Buenos Aires. It was terrible. He wanted to have another book translated—evidently it pays—but the man who translated the first book was incompetent. I found fourteen errors on one page. He translated 'Now' as 'No'—of course, perhaps he didn't see the 'w'. I wrote back that they should send me the proofs before they went to press. They only sent ten pages. I really thought the edition should be withdrawn, but they didn't do it."

"I thought a Spanish Count was your translator."

"The Marqués de Marichalar? Oh, he just translated the prologue and epilogue of THE LAST PURITAN . . . It was a very good selection, because it's a kind of frame to set off the rest. A lot of people think the story is about me—that I'm Oliver or Mario. It's not true. I was writing about my friends."

"But you did put some good things of yours into their talk," I insisted.

"Oh, in that sense, yes. And of course what was uppermost in my mind at the time was problems of friendship and marriage and religion. Even PERSONS AND PLACES," he added, "didn't come out as I wanted. I like marginal notes, and they had to be left out on account of the war. They also cut out the jokes—and some indiscretions."

I mentioned that I didn't care for Howgate's biography of him.

"Well, it's accurate. I found only one mistake, where he quoted someone else, saying I came to America in my fourteenth year. It was when I was eight and a half—my ninth. Howgate was just out of college—when was that?"

"The book appeared in 1936."

"It doesn't seem so long ago! I remember the past so clearly, but recent events get away from me. Howgate had never been out of the states. He didn't know Spain or England—I mean from the inside. I had come to love England more than I ever cared for America. He was interested in calling attention to himself in the academic world. At the time it appeared, the book was very complimentary. He handled my poetry very well, and gave a good account of my Life of Reason ... What did you have in mind doing?"

"Your biography."

"Where will you get the facts?"

"I hope to get some of them here. One reason I made the trip is to read the third part of Persons And Places."

"But it hasn't got dates—none of Persons And Places has dates."

"Well, of course, what I'm doing is part of that Bohemian series. I'm interested in giving an account of your ideas as part of a century-long movement. I'm including you in a series, along with Poe, Murger, George Sand, Verlaine and Rimbaud."

"I can't say I care too much for the company . . . Recently I've run into another Rimbaud—Lowell."

"Who?"

"Lowell, don't you know him? He won a Pulitzer prize."

I had to admit that the name was strange to me.

"Robert Lowell—he's one of my interests, and resembles Rimbaud."

"He must have got away from Boston."

"He broke with his family, and visited me in Europe—first time he'd been out. I have never found a young man with such a vocabulary. Reading his poems I had to use a dictionary. Some of the words I found, others I didn't." (Laughter.) "He may be in Rome any time now, with his wife—the second one. (More laughter.) "Of course, he's half crazy."

"Every now and then," he continued, "visitors come to see me. There was Corliss Lamont—you know him?"

I confessed that the philosopher was no friend of mine.

"I could hardly understand him. When there is more than one visitor I'm out of the conversation. And so many mumble. (I can understand *you*.) So many talk through their nose with a twang. (Santayana demonstrated.) Now, if Cory comes, it will be between you and him. I can't hear two people from a distance. Some time ago two young men called. When they were leaving I said if they came again I'd prefer their calling singly, so that I could talk with them properly. They never returned." This last in a slightly wistful note. "I suppose they were used to travelling together."

"Why don't you try a hearing-aid?" I queried.

"My doctor," he answered roguishly, "is Italian and Catholic. He speaks English, but we always talk Italian together. My Italian isn't good, but it's sufficient. My doctor has a Catholic idea that suffering may be good for one."

"I feel confined here," he added, "I used to go out, but now it's impossible. The taxis would knock me down. I do clean up in the room. They don't do it all for me. But when I stayed in hotels, I had several rooms. One hotel was torn down, but I also stayed at the Bristol. That was luxurious. You know, there are Bristols all over Italy. One of the first Englishmen to live in Italy was a Lord Bristol. He moved around a lot, and wherever he stayed it seems he laid an egg." (We laughed.)

"I could move," said Santayana," but I need so many things done for me now. Just the matter of stamps, for instance. I pay them by the month here, and they post my letters for me. I write a great many letters. I've thought of moving to some hotel again. How is the one where you are staying?"

"Old-fashioned, but nice."

"I miss an open fire. Has your room got one?"

"Yes. That is, it has a fireplace."

"At one hotel I only had two rooms. But the bath was nearby. You could almost call it your own."

"Possession is nine points of the law."

"Yes," he grinned, "*once* you get inside."

"There probably aren't many Englishmen in your hotel now," said Santayana, "but there must have been during the war. Even then they kept to themselves. Not the Americans! They were all over the place. They never looked as natty as the English. It was summer, and their uniforms were flimsy. They lounged around on every corner, and looked about as bad as I do now."

Santayana glanced down at his gray robe, which he wore over his trousers and shirt. The top of long underwear showed above the neck-line of his open collar, but the sage did not look shabby. I consulted my watch. An hour and a half had passed. All this time Santayana had sat at the foot of his chaise-longue with no back-rest. I feared he was tiring.

"You must dismiss me," I said, "when you feel tired. I can return tomorrow at any time you say."

"Oh," he exclaimed, "I get a lot of sleep. While I'm reading I often dream—sometimes it's hard to tell which is the dream and which is the waking state—"

"Nirvana?"

"No! But the sisters often find me here asleep, with a book still in my hand...Naturally, I repeat myself. People come whom I never see again, so I have my standard stories. They often ask how I came to this place."

"How did it happen?"

"I had tried a number of places. The natural one, of course, was Florence—there's where all the artists go—but the place is over-run by tourists. I tried Venice during one winter. Don't ever do it."

"Didn't you visit some small place in the Appenines?"

"The Dolomites—the Tyrolean Alps—:Cortina. I got there before anyone had arrived and stayed late. It's a summer resort

—cool and high—but the character of the place changed. I settled in Rome. When the war came, my money was cut to $100
a month. I can't live on that, you know, not even here. I tried
Switzerland, telling them that I could spend $500 a month in
their country. (I thought the war would last only a short time.)
You'd think it was to their advantage. But they didn't see it
that way. I'm a Spanish exile, and that looks bad."

"Maybe they thought you were a spy."

"In any case, I had some pocket money. So I asked the
sisters to take me in. I could pay the Chicago order, and the
Italians would never know. Now, I doubt if I shall ever leave."

"Before *I* leave," I interrupted, "I want to ask: What
would you do in my position, with seventeen days in Rome?"

"There are lots of places to visit."

"I don't mean that. I've been here before and have seen the
sights. If *you* were writing Santayana's biography . . ."

He had no suggestions to make. It is possible he did not catch
the drift of my question. I went on: "I should like very much
to read the last part of PERSONS AND PLACES as you wrote me I
could."

"Cory has a copy," he began, somewhat anxiously. "I don't
know if I have another. I could lend you Cory's copy—Cory
needn't know."

(I asked myself: *Who is this Cory?* and decided to meet
him.)

"This third part," said Santayana, rising, "is full of indiscretions. I'll look around. There should be another copy." He
walked over to a chest of drawers near the exit. "I'll start looking
right now," he said, "so that I don't forget."

I thanked him for the interview, and left him peering into
the top drawer, which was full of old papers and photographs. As
I departed I noticed a gilded Virgin on the chest of drawers.
Was it, I asked myself, a fixture of the clinic, or was it his?

MARCH 17, 1951

As I entered, Santayana was reading by a window.

"I have just been reading some of this with pleasure." He

held up the MS of Persons and Places, Part III. "I was reading about old Higgs." (An erratic tutor at Oxford, spoken of in this volume.) "Of course, two chapters have been published."

"I have read them," I said.

"Well, then, you won't need these." He removed two chapters. "It will lighten the weight you have to carry."

I thanked him and assured him nothing would happen to the copy.

"Cory has another," he said, "and then there's a manuscript copy—but I haven't been able to find it."

When I repeated that nothing would happen to this copy he said, "Oh, no. That's something one just dreams about. It won't happen."

"Don't Scribners have a copy?" I asked.

"No, these are all there are."

Santayana offered me several chairs. I took a small one and sat near him so that he could hear me. The light from the window fell full on my face. I decided afterwards that he had arranged it so—in order to see what I really looked like.

"Today was house-cleaning day," he volunteered. "Besides, I like to sit in the sun."

"Aren't you in a draft?"

"No. The other window is open. But I always like air. I never sleep with the window closed."

"I've brought along three things you might like to read," I said, "part of a chapter on Murger . . ."

"Who's he?"

"The one who wrote La Bohème—the novel. Also, the cosmological part of the book on Poe."

"I didn't know he had a cosmology. I must look at that."

"And a draft of an essay, An American Aristocracy?"

"Oh, don't get me wrong," he said, "I'm in favor of America for the Americans."

"This is just a speculative essay," I explained.

"Very well," he answered. I placed the folders on his desk.

"Also," I warned, "they're just drafts. You'll find quotations from you done from memory. I have to correct them."

"I'm not accurate," said Santayana. "I don't intend to be. I put down what I think it is, and start from there. It's a starting-point to get somewhere else."

Thereupon he showed me another illustration in Segreto Tibet. It was of a Dalai Lama in the act of intercourse with a beautiful woman—being one of several ritual panels photographed by the author. Underneath, Santayana had just written:

> *So once   the starlight drank the fire of love*
> *And Spirit knew the flesh that it was of.*

Below was a notation: "Cf.p.229 & Tav.44." This was Table 50. We turned to the other illustration. There sat the Dalai Lama, now in a more demure posture, alone on his throne.

"Do you know what Bhodisattvas are in the Buddhist religion?" Santayana asked.

"Yes. They're intermediaries between us and Nirvana."

"They are the ones who returned. This is how they represent it in Tibet: spirit in the arms of the flesh. (Doesn't he look German—with such a round face?) Yes, the Bhodhisattvas are mortals who reached Nirvana, then turned back to help others, and suffer in the flesh."

"They're *better* than the ones who enter Nirvana," I exclaimed—thinking at once of Santayana's Idea of Christ. "And the idea is like your notion of spirit."

He smiled but made no comment.

"I have some questions left over from yesterday," I said. "Was that *Percival* Lowell you mentioned, who was the poet?"

"No. *Robert*. Here are a couple of his books."

"Was his father the astronomer?"

"No, but I seem to remember that a Percival Lowell was an astronomer."

"Then Robert wasn't a Lowell of the Lowells."

"Oh, yes he was! And his father died recently, so now he

has something to live on . . . I knew James Russell slightly."

"And Lawrence?"

"Naturally. I even met Amy. She was elefantine."

"And smoked big cigars."

"But her poetry wasn't exactly virginal." (We laughed.) "I don't suppose she really had a lover, with those legs. She reminds me of two maiden ladies I knew—one in Paris, the other in Boston—who pretended to have lovers, but didn't!"

We laughed heartily at this, and the conversation proceeded in a jovial mood.

Santayana quoted at some length, in French, from L'ÉCOLE DES FEMMES; also from LES FEMMES SAVANTES. Two sisters argue whether they should be women or intellectuals, and each lectures the other: "We must obey our elders." Another passage, quoted verbatim, suggested that intelligence is not enough, at least in women.

After the fun died down I posed another question. "When you said yesterday that you'd like to see a refutation of the British school, beginning with Locke, did you include Whitehead?"

"No, not the important side of his philosophy: the symbolic —what did you call it yesterday?—(he chuckled)—semantic or romantic?—ah, yes!—not that side."

I assured him how kindly Whitehead had often spoken of him. He was always saying, "Read Santayana!" "Did you know him?" I inquired.

"Slightly. I was in the same room with him. He became a philosopher because he lost a son in the war—and his brother was a bishop." Santayana grinned. "That was Russell's theory, anyway." After laughing, Santayana frequently coughed, then spat into a glass dish on his desk.

Whitehead's life as a philosopher, I mentioned, probably began after his life as a teacher in England had ended. "I studied with him," I said, "and I also heard Russell. On the occasion of that talk, Whitehead introduced him. It was an odd performance. Whitehead was trying to be polite, but it seemed he disapproved of Russell."

"Russell has a very keen mind," Santayana said, "like a flashlight. He only sees one spot, and nothing exists beyond. All his life he has gone down the road with—what is their name?—ah! blinkers! However, I learned something from him. When he and Whitehead wrote the PRINCIPIA MATHEMATICA, I read the preface. Of course, I couldn't understand the mathematics, but I remember his explaining that you can have two infinities—one bigger than the other. Take a watch. You can divide an hour into an infinity of moments. But you can also divide each minute into an infinity. And yet one is bigger than the others!" Santayana laughed at this as if it were a capital joke.

After a pause, I raised an issue I had long had in mind. "In your system," I asked, "are essences and matter simply distinguished logically, by definition, or are they open to experiment?"

"They are categories. Experiment doesn't affect them. Essences are terms of thought—they point to something."

"Would you call them symbols?"

"I think terms is the better word."

"My reason for asking," I said, "is the recent development of electric calculating machines. They seem to resemble brain structures a good deal. You feed equations into them, and in a short time they come out with answers it would take 150 mathematicians 300 years to produce. A man at Massachusetts Institute of Technology, Norbert Wiener, is a leading figure. He calls it *cybernetics*, or the science of communication."

"I haven't heard of it."

"One of the big features, having a relation to your scheme, I think, is that although the thing works mechanically, the product is not mechanical; it's information. As Wiener says, information is information, and that's all."

"I see."

"But another point bears on what you call the material inefficacy of ideas. The energy needed to activate the little cells in these electric brains is negligible—because they are enclosed in an electric field. It suggests that one reason physiologists have never found a 'thought' is because the energy consumed is infinitesimal, and is buried in an electric field."

"The thought still requires a material base. It doesn't exist in a spiritual world of its own. Experiment makes no difference."

"I thought you would be interested."

"Of course it's interesting, but experiment doesn't change it. It's all a particular kind of motion." (Here he described a figure in the air.) "I was amused," he continued, "at Anaxagoras' notion of genesis, as if matter didn't contain spirit potentially from the beginning. He uses the old idea that like begets like, that you can't get something different—when it happens all the time. My system is more like Bergson's in that respect. Strike a match. The flame isn't the match! It's a new essence. Of course, if you're speaking of chemical molecules, they're the same—but at a different level . . ."

"That reminds me," I said, "of what Hu Shih wrote about Americans."

Santayana did not recognize the name. I quoted Hu Shih as saying that Americans, because they did not resign themselves to matter, as Orientals do, but used it for their own purposes,. were more spiritual."

"But that's animal," Santayana objected vivaciously. "That's just being an animal. They use that to refute materialism. They say mind created all that machinery. But what did mind use— more mind?"

I let the matter drop. Santayana coughed occasionally, and I had the feeling he was under the weather. I determined to leave earlier than yesterday. Also, I felt I was pulling the weight of the conversation. Santayana seemed more passive, as if waiting for what I should ask next.

"I've been wondering," I said, "whether as I pass through Boston on my way home, I should stop at the Harvard library and read your thesis on Lotze."

"Oh, no. I did that because I had to."

"Still, as a youthful work . . ."

"I wanted to do Schopenhauer, but Royce said it wouldn't be suitable for a doctoral dissertation. I liked Schopenhauer at the time. Even at Avila I had a copy, and my father found it. 'What do you want this for?' he asked. He couldn't read German, so he thought it was useless."

"I had also considered looking up some back files of the LAMPOON for your cartoons," I said.

"They're no good. Most of the subjects were suggested to me. But the first one, about the ladies trying to get a room at Holyoke House for class-day was my idea. I sent it in. The editors got in touch with me, saying they wanted to keep it and print it later. There were many hotels called Holyoke in those times . . . Most of the other subjects were suggested to me. The cartoons were poor. I had no touch. My father said the design was good, but there was no touch."

"I saw one or two pictures of you in LIFE. You played leading lady in the *Hasty Pudding* show, didn't you?"

"That was a mistake. It wasn't the Pudding show, but another:—the Lady Papillonetta. That was in my junior year, I believe. I was almost class-day orator, but I wasn't quite good enough. At Harvard I won several second prizes in declamation. I was always winning second prizes. At the Boston Latin School I won a prize for Latin declamation."

Here he began to quote from the second book of the AENIAD, but had to give it up. "The words don't come," he explained, "but just the other day I was saying them over to myself."

I noticed that some spots from the previous meal were visible on the sage's shirt.

"Then at the Latin School," he went on, "I was made Colonel, because I was more representative of the school than a fellow named Weston, who had received one more vote in the election. I went to the Head-master—said I didn't think it was quite right. He asked if I objected too much. I said, No— so Weston was left out. His father protested to the Head-master, said it was undemocratic, and that his son was as good as anybody else. He took him out of school. Weston never said anything to me, and I was indifferent. All it would have meant was that he would be Colonel and I should be Major."

"Duron says in his book that you were Colonel because of your physical agility. Did you go in for sports?"

Santayana smiled. "No. I was just big for my age, and more representative, they thought. Since then I've shrunk."

"How tall are you?"

"Five feet seven."

"I was interested," I proceeded, "in a remark of yours that the life of the mind needs protection from the secular arm."

"It does."

"Then you think it can be institutionalized?"

"Oh, it *has* to be, if you are to prevail. Just look at what the Moslems did in a few years. They conquered and converted. The only thing that held them together was religion. They had no race-prejudice. That's why they had such success among the Negroes. The Persians were a different sect, but also influential."

"Look at what the Spaniards did," I said, "to the Incas."

"I imagine all immigrants to the United States are assimilated," he contended, "even where you live."

"No," I replied. "The situation is somewhat different in San Antonio. We're right next to the old culture—bombarded by it through movies and radio. The old ties are stronger than among immigrants up north, who were cut off completely from the old country."

"I imagine the Mexicans try to assimilate themselves," Santayana suggested. "After all, it's only natural. You don't want to be different."

"Well," I admitted, "there's a powerful bribe offered—gold!"

"You can't blame them . . . Then, of course, look what the Russians are doing. I was reading about a man in a cell—not (he laughed) like this one—a party cell, you know: five members. It reminded me of the catechism. When they got a message from up above, one of them would read it to the others, and then have each one say it. If a dull man with a good memory could repeat it exactly, he'd be told, 'You've got it right!' " Santayana laughed heartily at this, and glanced at me to see if I enjoyed the joke as much as he.

"Well," I went on," there is some question in my mind whether institutions are a good or an evil, in education at least. My dad has been in public education all of his life and so have I, both day and night-schools . . ."

"Oh," Santayana interposed quickly, "evening-schools!" (There was a touch of scorn in his voice.) "The school has to stand for something in the community. Ours did. Of course we didn't have all the sports—no football, but we had base-ball . . ."

I had found out what I wished, so remained silent. Santayana sighed, "Ah, yes—childhood!"

I picked up my things.

"Is it so cold out?" he asked. "You're wearing a coat and a scarf."

"Last night when I returned it was chilly."

"It's a very nice coat," he commented.

It had troubled me to be invisible to him, save as a floating apparition.

"Here's a passport picture," I said, handing him one, "so you can know what I look like."

"But it doesn't look like you," he exclaimed unexpectedly. "The features are set, while yours are so mobile."

"In any case," I replied, "from now on I won't be a blob on the landscape."

Thanking him again for the MS, I departed.

MARCH 18, 1951

"*Avanti!*" said Santayana as I knocked. I thought he was conversing with someone, but found him alone, just awake from a doze on the chaise-longue.

"I woke you," I said. "I'm sorry."

"It's nothing. I had a rather bad night—indigestion, and then I have a cold all the time: chronic catarrh. When you get old, those things take hold."

"I hope I didn't bring you a germ from the United States."

"Oh, no," he laughed, but I noticed he motioned me to sit across the table from him. I myself had developed a cold—whether from shouting at him for an hour and half yesterday or for some other reason. It was quite possible that we had given each other trans-Atlantic colds.

"I've been reading *you* this morning," he began. "Two of them I couldn't read. The print was so faint. But I read most of the Murger. I found several mistakes."

"I'm sure you did," I said. "It's only a draft and the quotations were done from memory. I appreciate your finding them."

"I marked them," he said. "One of mine is wrong. I never said that—in fact, I shouldn't."

We tracked down the culprit. I had written: "a century-long thaw in human feeling." (I had been thinking of this, from page two of PERSONS AND PLACES: "The general thaw . . . of that age."

"Then that quotation from Shakespeare, it doesn't go that way. It makes a line, and you don't have a line."

The quotation was about giving airy nothings a local habitation and a name.

"I know," I said, "that was all to be checked."

"As for style, it isn't the way I should write it," said Santayana, "but I can't judge. I'm fifty years behind the times. We had conventions that aren't followed now. Of course, they were just customs."

By no means embarrassed by criticism from one of the world's greatest stylists, I said, "I'm no prose writer. However, I don't intend putting out the first book of the series until the last is finished. The whole set is to be revised.

"Oh, it's to be several books?"

"Yes."

"This idea of intellectuals as a class, you don't mean all

the intellectuals?"

"I was dealing with the Bohemians."

"Well, there were many others. Bohemia was mainly painters . . ."

"Oh, no! Murger and all those I treated were writers, novelists, and the like."

"But they weren't all poor. There were intellectuals in other circles. Some of them knew something."

"Murger's Bohemia was just one. Baudelaire's Bohemia was called the *Bohème galante* or *dorée*. It included Gautier, Barbey d'Aurevilly, Nerval, and—the author of Les Caryatides . . ." (I afterward remembered the name: Banville.)

"That sounds classical."

"They were! The aristocratic *Bohème* imitated classical models—at first."

"It seems to me that many were victims of circumstances."

I let that pass. The point of the series is just so: that Bohemians are not Bohemians from choice—not even Santayana.

"I see you mention Sartre."

"Yes, but I don't feel competent to include him in the series. In fact, his work falls outside the period I'm treating: 1830-1930. Now, *you* fall in that period."

"Oh, yes."

"But I see you as a kind of doorway out of Bohemia— you transcend it."

"I was in Paris quite a time, you know. I had the use of Strong's apartment when he was in America." (Charles Augustus Strong had been a college friend and a life-long philosophical colleague.)

"That was around 1906?"

"Yes, when I lectured at the Sorbonne."

"You lived there later again, didn't you—around the thirties?"

"The late twenties or early thirties."

"It must have been around the time you gave that lecture on Locke in London. My friend, Dr. Dodson, met you then in

Paris. You must have been at some side-walk café. Of course you
don't remember him."

"No."

I repeated the incident mentioned in the Introduction.

"I never attend those (*philosophical*) conventions," Santayana commented, as he had so many years before to my friend.
This, I thought to myself, from the man who claims that learning
should be institutionalized. Or possibly he does not hope to
"prevail!"

"Even here in Rome I didn't go," Santayana continued. "I
sent a paper, but I didn't want to. However, Paris is a fine
city. I got to know *Montmartre* and across the river where the
Bohemians moved—what's its name?"

"*Montparnasse?*"

"Yes. It's true what you say of the Bohemians moving out
where they can be alone. I got to know other circles too. I'm
a conservative, you know, and Bohemians are radicals."

Again I let it pass. Murger, arch-Bohemian, was an arch-
conservative, like Baudelaire, except in his impetuous youth.
But I was not in Rome to convert the Pope.

"I once attended an anti-Dreyfus meeting," Santayana said.
"I forget who invited me. Then on another occasion I was
invited to a dinner meant to bring about a reconciliation of
two enemies. There was a long table. The host and hostess sat
across from each other at the middle. The two enemies sat at
opposite ends. They had greeted each other on entering, but the
conversations at both ends of the table were completely separate.
I sat in the middle next to the hostess, and heard both."

How fantastically symbolic of Santayana! I reflected.

"You must know a lot of the French writers," he burst
out suddenly.

"No," I said. "I took French every year at Harvard under
Professor Morize, but other than that, it's been these Bohemians."

He subsided into one of his waiting moods.

"As usual," I said, "I have some left-over questions—for

one, what was that Professor's name in Honolulu?"

"Moore—I'll look up his first name, if you like." Santayana started to get out of his chaise-longue.

"No, no!" I protested. "I'll find it. There's a reference to him in Northrop's book."

I then asked for a list of *all* Spanish translations of his works.

"I never know," he said. "It makes them angry that I won't give them exclusive rights, but one of my friends in Spain might want to translate something."

I asked what there was besides THE IDEA OF CHRIST and the prologue and epilogue of THE LAST PURITAN.

"The second part of PERSONS AND PLACES is around here somewhere," he said. "I couldn't ask for a better translation. The first part I don't have at the moment, but it's just as good."

"It's a Buenos Aires publisher?"

"Yes, *Editorial Sud America.*"

We went on to discuss how rare some of his books have become.

"Pearsall Smith," said Santayana, "got me an English connection: Constable. They were supposed to have reprinted two things: WINDS OF DOCTRINE and EGOTISM IN GERMAN PHILOSOPHY."

I said I had obtained the first.

"The second seems to have had quite a success during this war. The British are slowly beginning to accept it. In the first war they criticized it. They said I was taking advantage of the situation to attack the wonderful German philosophy. Now they've had a little more of that wonderful German philosophy." He laughed.

"Pound came to see me," he said suddenly.

"Ezra Pound?"

"Yes. He got an introduction from Cory—not necessary, of course. He thought I might help him with THE REALM OF SPIRIT. He tried to make it clear to me. It was about those cantos. There were to be a hundred, with a rose at the end, like Dante's—an apotheosis. I don't think it helped him. I can't understand his poetry."

"Some of the translations are good—from the Chinese."

"Yes, but he says anyone can do them. He doesn't like them. Everybody tells me you mustn't try to understand modern poets, just feel. But I'm afraid they don't know exactly what they feel, so they can't put it down. Even T. S. Eliot seems vague at times."

"Well," I laughed, "what do you expect? When a man goes in for all sorts of languages, and in English verse! Even Sanskrit: Da, Datta!—you remember, in The Waste Land."

"It means God," said Santayana. (T. S. Eliot, in a note, says that this fragment of the Upanishads means: "Give, Sympathise, Control.")

We talked then about other rare volumes of Santayana's. I mentioned the 35¢ editions of Whitehead's and Langer's work. He said he had never heard of such editions. (Later, I noticed several on his book-shelves.) He seemed impressed when I made a plea for poor students who couldn't afford to pay $6 for every philosophy text.

"Of course, conditions may be more crowded," he said, "but when I was a student we could go to the library or take books out."

I assured him that that could still be done, but when everybody in a class needs the text? He agreed that a new edition of The Life of Reason was needed, in one volume, and said that the one-volume edition of Realms of Being was the best. I had not seen the purple-bound Triton edition, which he pointed out to me on his shelves.

"One thing, having nothing to do with your philosophy as such," I said, "is causing it to be noticed."

"What is that?"

"Your steadfastness. A strong will hypnotises weak wills. Most people have no fixed opinions. Eventually they are bound to come round to yours. As for me, I'm from another generation. To me your principles seem self-evident."

"To me also, but I don't expect anyone to agree with me.

Very few people are without a country. They're not uprooted. They couldn't stand it. And it's not good, you know."

Here a momentary sadness seemed to cross his face, as he shot me a searching glance.

"Do you know Prall?" I asked.

"Prall?"

"He has made a reputation in the United States as your follower."

"Never heard of him."

"Well," I said, "when I returned to Harvard in 1933 I met him. We talked about aesthetics. He asked me what I thought was the best work on it. 'Santayana,' I said. 'Yes,' he answered. 'I tried to use THE SENSE OF BEAUTY once as a text, but the students couldn't understand it.' "

"Why," exclaimed Santayana, "there's nothing in it. It's a young lady's idea of art. Nowadays they teach it at girls' schools."

I laughed.

"My verses, too," he added.

"Oh, no!"

"If you want an anecdote about me," he said—and proceeded to retell the Bryn Mawr episode found in PERSONS AND PLACES. "I had a bald spot in back," Santayana admitted.

I brought the conversation back momentarily to the subject of cheap editions, saying, "Students never have much money, as you know yourself."

"No," he agreed, "and when I was at Cambridge we had no water in our rooms; you had to bring it up. But I always managed to have a fire in a hearth."

He reminisced some about Harvard and Prescott Street, where he had lived.

"Someone wrote me," he said, "from Prescott Street. Was it you?"

"No."

"Did I dream it? Often I find little difference between waking and dreaming." He finally remembered the man, a teacher at Harvard.

"I detested Boston!" I exclaimed.

"I didn't," he rejoined. "I rather liked it. Of course there are better places to live, but many worse."

I mentioned Philadelphia.

"No," he said. "I didn't care too much for Philadelphia. I was there in 1875."

At this he laughed heartily. He might as well have said he had visited Benjamin Franklin.

"My mother sent my brother Robert and me to the exposition—why, I don't know. She was quite poor."

"She believed in progress," I suggested.

"Yes, she did—and I suppose she wanted us to see the city. I was sick—indigestion—part of the time. I didn't see too much. We stayed at an old Sturgis house. The upper rooms were empty."

Here followed an elaborate description of a typical Philadelphian home, with rooms off the stairway landings between floors.

"I've always been interested in houses," said Santayana. He went on to mention the white shutters common in his time on Philadelphian homes.

"The Quaker influence?" I asked.

"I don't know."

I mentioned having noticed little bridges over front courtyards.

"Yes," Santayana laughed. "You could close the shutters, pull up the drawbridge and flood the cellar. You would be safe. No one could attack you!"

With his usual sense of style, I realized, Santayana was terminating by means of a witty phrase a theme which threatened to grow dull. I changed the subject.

"There are a number of myths which have grown up about you," I said.

"No doubt."

"I want to see if there's anything to them. LIFE, TIME and

other papers make out a rather unfavorable picture of you, which dismays me and distresses me."

"It distresses me too. They never use my own words."

"I guessed as much."

I retold several absurdities, ending with a recent Detroit clipping which had said he wasn't worried about Communism: if it conquered Europe, western thought would conquer it.

"In several hundred years, yes," said Santayana. "But in the meantime? You could be thrown in prison. You could be tortured. What I meant was that ours isn't the only civilization. It's just habit. It's bound to change."

"Why does everybody that interviews you talk about Communism?"

"It's in the air. I object more when they interview me about Fascism. Edman came determined to make me out a Fascist."

"Well," I asked, "how about that story when you were said to have walked out of the lecture-room at Harvard into the spring?" One writer had quoted him as saying on that occasion, "I have a rendezvous with spring"—after which he was seen very little at Harvard.

"That wasn't true. I used to tell a story about William James, who became restless at one of his lectures. The man obviously wanted to get away, and he looked out of the windows at the spring greenery. Finally, he left, but there was nothing said, as is attributed to me."

"Another story," I went on, "is how you are reputed to read books. It was said you tear the page out after you're finished and throw it away. I expected to wade through paper when I entered your room."

"I don't do that. Sometimes, when I went walking, I didn't care to take all of a cheap edition along, so I'd cut out 32 pages— two sections— and put them in my pocket. On my desk there you'll see a heavy German book on Alexander the Great. I've cut it up because it's too heavy to hold . . . One Italian journalist interviewed me. I like to sew, you know—that is, buttons, and mend things that are torn. I do little things around the room, so as not to read all the time. Well, in summer I would wear pyjamas with an open collar—I'm not fifty years behind in everything, you see—(we laughed)—I had mended a tear in the collar. The journalist reported that I received him in old pyjamas darned at the collar!"

"Newspapers seem to want to cast things you do in the wrong light," I said "This story, that even I retold, about your receiving charity from the nuns wasn't true at all, apparently."

"It wasn't true at the beginning. But the Italian government found out about the Chicago arrangement—I'm rather ashamed of what happened—and after two months stopped the $100 coming in. After that, till the war was over, I only had my 30,000 Lire for pocket money, so you see it was charity as far as this establishment was concerned. At the armistice I owed them $7000, but the government wouldn't allow me to pay this hospital. I arranged to send monthly payments to the Chicago branch. The money helped greatly because they were making repairs at the time. Finally, through a man in Boston named Appleton—he's my trustee, now that my nephew is dead—some of my money isn't mine directly, it's in trust—sent me 70,000 Lire. What was I to do with that? I told the sisters I would open a bank account— something I never did here before—and pay my daily expenses out of it for about three years. I never imagined I'd be here ten."

From this war experience, Santayana went on to explain, he had developed niggardly habits. "I'm not niggardly in big things, but in small things the habit remains." Among other habits left over from this time, he said, was that of cutting his own hair. "I like to do little things," he repeated. I asked if he used clippers. "Oh, no," he replied. "I don't like clippers— I never did. I used scissors." And he demonstrated how, with scissors, he cut his own hair—of which, fortunately, very little remained.

Looking at my watch I saw that two hours had almost passed. Several questions were still on my mind.

"When you said, in OBITER SCRIPTA, that you wished you could begin in your philosophy where you had left off, what did you have in mind?"

"I meant that if I could have started with my present system, I could have stated its applications more clearly. As it was, I had to go by instinct and feeling. I knew what I *didn't* like. I criticized other philosophers, in spots, though I didn't know them well."

(I smiled at this modesty.)

"I gave classes in the history of philosophy. I tried to make them sympathetic. The trouble was, when it came to what I *liked*, I was sympathetic with many points of view." (Here was Santayana with his ultimate relativity.)

"One thing more," I said. "Are there any pictures you would care for me to have photostated for my book?"

"A portrait?"

"Or any family photographs that you might think appropriate. My other books are going to have a number of illustrations."

"There aren't any family portraits here."

"Perhaps of Russell?—anything like that. I'm asking now, because it takes time to photostat things, and I could have it done here."

He seemed doubtful. "I intended to issue a new edition of all three parts of PERSONS AND PLACES," he said, "with illustrations."

"And the omitted paragraph headings, I hope," said I. "Last night I finished reading the third part."

"You *finished!*" Santayana exclaimed incredulously.

"Yes, I sat up late, and only got up at twelve. That's an overview, of course."

"Why, the one chapter on travels is long in itself. I don't see how . . . but then, some people read fast."

"I do."

"Did you read about the *Euthanasia of Molly?*" This was an amusing paragraph heading, omitted from the present edition of MY HOST THE WORLD.

"Yes," I replied.

"Would you like to see her picture?"

"By all means."

Santayana rose and began looking through suit-cases and drawers. An Italian journalist, he said, had made fun of his nineteenth century Gladstone and kit-bags.

"He said they were from the 70's. They're from the 80's."

"At least you're not a carpet-bagger," I laughed. "And incidentally, this Virgin here: is it yours or did it come with the place?"

"Everything here, besides my books, is the Sisters'." The *décor* of the room included a crucifix, hanging next to one window over a cloth screen, and pages of religious illustrations, which Santayana had rolled up and used as a lamp-shade. "If I had known," he said, "that I was going to be here ten years, I'd have brought some furnishings with me."

He had found an envelope of photographs and took them over to the desk. He drew out a photo-postcard, blazoned: *Woman Suffrage*.

"Here's Molly," he said.

The caption identified her as Lady Russell.

"She's exactly as you described her," I commented.

"Yes, standing at the speaker's stand, waiting for the applause to die down *before* she speaks," he chuckled.

"And this is Russell," he said, "—at his best."

"He doesn't look like his brother, Bertrand."

"No, he was big. Here's Russell at his worst."

I saw a figure with an obvious paunch. This dated, I knew, from only eight years later.

"He looks as if he were imitating Teddy Roosevelt," I said.

"Oh, no, but he changed quickly."

"Was Jim Darnley, in THE LAST PURITAN, Lord Russell?" I inquired.

"Yes," Santayana gasped. "How did you know *that?*"

"I didn't. I just guessed."

(I had put two and two together, long before my trip. Reading the third part of PERSONS AND PLACES had confirmed me in this and other conjectures.)

"Yes," Santayana repeated, "it was Russell."

He brought forth a number of photostats of a recent portrait of himself by Lipinsky.

"Could I have one for a frontispiece?" I cried.

"Yes, you can have one if you like, but for a frontispiece I prefer another."

He brought out the frontispiece of his Triton edition.

"I insisted on this for the Triton edition," he said. "It was done when I was thirty-four. It shows all sides of my character, they say—the good and the bad. Now this," (he held up the recent likeness) "shows only one—of course, I'm not so many-sided."

"Oh, no?" I objected. "This makes you look like Gandhi."

"That's the side one ought to emphasize. Cory says it looks like me when I'm listening to someone."

This was true. When Santayana talks his smile and teeth give him a faun-like expression.

"An artist here did an oil painting of me. You can't show all sides at once. That one is gross—gross."

He apparently had no copy of this. I remarked about my plan to write a novel, Maya, wherein one individual looks different to many persons and where even two portraits of the same man fail to resemble one another.

He handed me a copy of the portrait by Lipinsky. "Would you like to wrap that up?" he asked.

I accepted and thanked him again, promising to return tomorrow.

"I'm afraid I shan't be able to read all of your writing," he said, "on account of my eyes."

"That's all right," I said, "—whatever you feel up to."

As I walked toward the Colosseum a drizzling rain began. I glanced at my package. It was the wrapper, identified in Santayana's own script, of "*Persons and Places, Vol. III. Typwritten copy*." With so precious a bit of autography under my arm, I wondered if even the great man himself realized how, as carelessly as he had handed me this bit of paper, he had imparted to me the key to his enigmatic novel.

MARCH 19, 1951

I knocked and received no answer. I waited, thinking some ablutions might be in progress. Silence. I knocked again. Finally, a familiar voice spoke: *"Avanti."*

Santayana sat by the left window in his arm-chair, obviously just roused from a nap.

"I came later today," I began, "so that you could get a nap, and here I've awakened you from deep sleep after all."

"No matter."

"Did you have a bad night? I'm afraid I wore you out yesterday."

"Oh, no. I had a good night. What is that portfolio you have under your arm?"

"I'll explain in a moment. It requires a proper introduction." I set down a large cardboard folder, and took off my coat.

"Today I don't intend to stay long," I explained. "Talking two hours straight with me every day must be a marathon."

"I have nothing to do," said Santayana. "Nowadays I eat less than ever and seem to sleep all the time."

A letter lay on his table. "I want you to look at this letter," he said. I glanced at the outside.

"It looks like your handwriting," I remarked.

"Open it."

Inside, in an outlandish script, I read:

S. Eliz

Sometime   DC
    in March

Dear G S
        What about that book
        of yours? Are your ————ishers
        trying to suppress yr/
        indecorous opinions, ?

or only the usual
American tempo—molasses
flowing up hill below zero

Cordially yr.

E z P

"It's from Ezra Pound," Santayana explained. "This is comparatively normal. Read the side."

On one flap of the combined envelope and letter, Pound had written:

"Qt. fr J. Dennison Re/Colby."

"Colby is the editor of the SATURDAY REVIEW," Santayana interpreted. The quote ran: "So He Kom to Me To Find out wot His Kerakter wuz." Ref. Daily Mail.

We examined the letter for its curious orthography.

"He even signs it, 'cordially yours'," Santayana commented. "Very commonplace. These Bohemians are usually more radical . . . But what did you bring in that portfolio?"

"This," I said with a flourish, "holds the secret of the atom-bomb. I told them so when I went through the Spanish customs, but they let me in anyway."

I unfolded my package. "A friend asked me to bring you this. He also offered to send you his copy of Jeffers' poems, but I couldn't accept that. It was a presentation copy. Now I am discharging my commission. This is called mobile sculpture."

"Is it a fan?" asked Santayana, as I proceeded to unpack.

"No, you hang it up and it blows in the wind. Of course, to you, with your bad eyesight, I know it will seem a white elephant. But we foresaw all that. 'If Santayana cares as little for material things as I think he does,' my friend assured me, 'tell him to give it to the Sisters. Someone will enjoy having it in his room.' Wounded soldiers during the war got awfully tired looking at the same spider day after day on the ceiling." I held the mobile suspended.

"Why, it's a toy," said Santayana. "If I hung that up people would know I was crazy."

"A toy for adults," I conceded.

"It's like a kaleidescope."

(I recalled just reading in Part Three of PERSONS AND PLACES how Santayana liked kaleidescopes—but no: that was off on a wrong tack.)

"Oh, it moves by itself. Does it create air-currents?"

"It's non-mechanical movement," I explained. "The wind moves it. You enjoy it as you might a limb swinging in the breeze. My friend has a translucent screen at home. Mobiles made of plastic cast shadows on it in color. You have repetition, but endless variation within it. You might say they are to space what music is to sound."

Mischievously, Santayana volunteered, "It creates the air currents by which it moves?" (This remark had many overtones to one knowing his philosophy.)

"No," I said, "the wind moves it."

"And you brought me this," said Santayana, amazed, "all the way from the United States?"

"Yes, and I nearly lost it in Madrid."

"I never know what people are going to give me next. One lady sent me a book: FORTY WAYS OF MAKING LOVE."

"We had you figured out from your last letter," I said, "—alone in an empty cell. But this is by no means a cell and it's far from empty, so you must do as you like with the mobile." I began to repack it.

"The book, FORTY WAYS OF MAKING LOVE, sounded exciting," Santayana continued," but it was just verses and they weren't very good. I had to pack it away in the grip over there so that the Sisters wouldn't get the wrong idea."

"Where shall I put this?" I asked.

"The room is so full now," he stammered. "Oh, well, put it behind the grip."

I placed it near FORTY WAYS OF MAKING LOVE.

"To whom am I indebted for this?" Santayana asked.

"Fred Dreher, from St. Louis."

"I once knew a man named Dreher," Santayana said, and his voice trailed away uncertainly . . . "Mr. Cardiff, from Yakima,

Wisconsin . . ."

"You mean Washington?"

"Yes, of course, Yakima, Washington—once wrote, asking for atoms of my thought."

"Atoms?"

(I presume the connection was my remark about the atomic bomb.)

"Haven't you seen the book? It's a collection of sayings from my work. It's over on the shelf there, next to the purple volumes."

I found a book, published in 1950 by the Philosophical Library, ATOMS OF THOUGHT, compiled by Ira D. Cardiff.

"Cory," Santayana explained, "has a collection of my last poems that gave Cardiff the idea for the title. One poem speaks of 'atoms of light.' I call the collection POSTHUMOUS POEMS. Cory will print it when I die."

I leafed through the volume, then set it down.

"Cardiff left out the funny sayings," Santayana said, "but I suppose that's Yakima. It sounds Japanese."

"Indian," I said.

"It was quite complimentary of him to do it. He wrote that it was time more people got to know my work. The trouble is, they'll stop with the sayings. I wrote Cardiff that his selection seemed to make me out more leftish than I am. I'm a conservative, a Tory. These people feel radical. Of course, I feel myself advanced, but for them it's in the past."

(*Timocracy*, I thought to myself.)

"Has the book any organization?" I asked, rising to look at it again.

"Oh, it's organized. There's an index."

"From harlots," I said, reading from the index, "to Zanzibar" —the last being my own invention.

"Cardiff wanted me to suggest twelve sayings he had left out. I suggested one or two, but I don't want to be responsible. I should have thought he would have put in the definition of poetry and religion, from INTERPRETATIONS OF POETRY AND

RELIGION." Santayana quoted this. "The longest saying is from
THE LAST PURITAN. A jewel-merchant is talking about women—
I forget his name . . ."

"Boskowitz?"

"Ah, Boskowitz!—Something to the effect that you can't
go wrong with good women. You see, he wants Mario to marry
his daughter. He says something about her body being like a
flower and her soul like a jewel. But you see, that's not I talking
—that's Boskowitz! Now, if he had taken what Mario says . . ."

"Ha!" I thought to myself. "This from the man who said
he was none of his characters." My private opinion was that,
virtually, Santayana is *both* Oliver in his spiritual side and Mario
in his carnal side—with many other transmutations, incarnations,
and disguises, including some of the women.

"If he had taken Mario's saying about telling truth to women,
that would have been mine. You know: where he says that if
you change the truth a little you can remember it better." (He
laughed and eyed me to see if I appreciated his humor.)
"Perhaps Cardiff's too serious," he concluded.

"Oh, no!" I protested. "Really serious people know how to
laugh."

"Well, then, maybe he's not serious."

"How important," I finally inquired, "is this epigrammatic
style of yours. It seems to be the first thing people mention,
and often they never get beyond it."

"When I was younger, I read a lot of Latin—: Latin epi-
grams. They came easily to me then. I can't write them any
longer. I've got away from that."

"This book by Pearsall Smith"—an anthology—"is it important?"

"It's a serious attempt. At the time he made the collection
it was a very kind thing for him to do. I helped him with it,
you know."

"What kind of a person was Smith—an aesthete?"

"Fastidious—interested in little things. He was very helpful,
getting Constable to publish my books. Scribners published

nothing in the States from the time of THE LIFE OF REASON until very recently. The American editions were from Constable's sheets."

"I was wondering about Smith. He wrote in UNFORGOTTEN YEARS that anthologizing is such a 'dainty art'. I didn't care for that. Does he understand the big ideas, the architecture?"

"Smith wasn't interested in my philosophy when it came to argument. He was interested in prose style. Of course, I don't argue much."

This was true. Santayana is on the side of intuition, not logic.

"Smith wanted to write beautiful prose. Some of it is. He was afraid, however, of making mistakes, so it isn't strong. And then he lived in England and was surrounded by English conventions. TRIVIA is good. And there's a good part in UNFORGOTTEN YEARS, about the American poet—now, what is the man's name?"

"Whitman?"

"Yes. Smith and his mother called on Whitman and his wife, or that woman he was living with. She said, 'Walt, there are *carriage people* downstairs.'" (Santayana guffawed.)

I recognized that a paragraph in our conversation was evidently at an end. Still thinking, apparently, of persons who had quoted him, Santayana continued: "Edman came to interview me once, and I made him very angry."

"The Edman who interviewed you and tried to make you out a Fascist? Irwin Edman, the philosopher?"

"Yes. He's Jewish and a pragmatist. I made the mistake of saying I didn't like Dewey. Edman was horribly disappointed. He had taken a great liking to my works—could quote whole passages from them, and here I was on the side of the devil." (Laughter.)

"I also criticized William James. James was interested in preserving free-will, the importance of making your own decisions—indeterminacy. Not physical indeterminacy—: spiritual. You see, he was good, and wanted to take the credit. I was bad, and so I enjoyed not being held responsible." This was the occasion for prolonged laughter by both of us.

"James was very kind to me," Santayana went on seriously," but he never understood me." Here followed the explanation as given in PERSONS AND PLACES.

"Perry has published some of your letters to James, hasn't he?" I asked.

"Oh, but they're very old. I was James' student at the time. I had a fellowship in Berlin. They gave me $500 a year, so I had to report regularly on what I was doing. I had $500 of my own, and with another $500 I could live, but not without it. You see, it was very important to keep them in a good humor."

"Both you and Whitehead, it seems to me," I said, "derive a great deal of your theory of feeling and emotion from James. You know: one feels sad because he cries . . ."

"James was originally a medical man. I found him most interesting when he was very young, with his medical illustrations. He was very well educated. He had been in Germany and France and spoke the languages like a native. In later years, it seemed to me his French grew worse—or my ear had become more sensitive."

"It gets away, if one doesn't practice." (I was going to mention my own speaking of German when a child, but refrained, remembering Santayana's prejudice—as I then thought—against Germany.)

"James knew the French Protestant writers and quoted them often," Santayana said. "I found one, Rénouvier, useful in my classes later. He wrote a history of philosophies. I never saw them so patly distinguished."

"That's Gallic."

"Another gentleman came to see me," Santayana remembered, "from here. He paid me a great compliment. He brought a copy of PERSONS AND PLACES and read me a paragraph about Spinoza that he liked. It was the line where I say that Spinoza is completed by the Greeks, and the Greeks by Spinoza. I was telling about the lectures I heard in Berlin by Paulsen . . . This man was a radical who came to see me . . . Actually, Bergson was right: change *is* fundamental. Have you read Bergson?"

"Creative Evolution."

"Matière et Mémoire is better—at least I think so, and his last book. But what Bergson doesn't allow for is tropes. They're natural too—a circular movement that doesn't change. It's just as natural for nature to remain the same, for a limited period, as for it to change."

I mentioned Jeffer's poem, Nova, wherein the sun blows up.

"Ah, well, over thousands of light-years, aeons, yes—change is inevitable. But people don't have to change, only gradually."

What, I inquired, did he think of the future of Christianity?

"It will last for aeons," he replied, "as long as the human race."

"Do you think it will undergo transformation?"

"Undoubtedly. Eventually we may find Heaven here on earth."

"I think you have never done anything better," I said, "than Ultimate Religion."

Vehemently Santayana exclaimed, "I wrote that from the heart!"

"Howgate tells about your reading it at a convention in The Hague, and how a German who didn't understand English was nevertheless impressed, just by the tone of your voice."

"By the tone of my voice? Ah, yes. Pollock was there—an old man of ninety. When he was younger he had written on Spinoza. He's a very important writer, of course. On this occasion, since he was hard of hearing, they put him near me. There was a table, with a light over it, and next to me sat Pollock. I put him to sleep! He slept through the entire speech, but I woke him up at the end. Where I say 'Sursum Corda,' etc. from the mass, I raised my voice so that everyone should hear the Latin. That woke him up. He pretended he had heard the whole speech."

"Platonism and the Spiritual Life," Santayana continued, "was another book I wrote almost at one sitting—up in Cortina. It started out as a review of Inge's Plotinus, but it got away from me. I am very fond of it. Constable was quite nice. He bound it in black at my request—like a prayer-book. I suppose it's out of print now."

"I wasn't able to get it. The edition of A HERMIT OF CARMEL was quite beautiful."

"Oh, that was a mistake! I should never have reprinted it. I left it out of the collected poems. It was a step in the wrong direction. I should have eliminated most of the collected poems too."

"Oh, no!"

"Well, since you are writing a kind of psychological study of my ideas, you should read them, but they were a false step. A great deal of THE LIFE OF REASON was a false step too. I shouldn't have written it. You'll find my philosophy in REASON IN ART, but it's not about art. I use 'art' in the sense of economic and liberal art—broadly."

"Crafts?"

"Some of my friends say that I should have called them useful and fine arts—but that's just the point. A useful art—an economic art—can become a liberal art if a man puts his heart in it, and isn't working for money."

"One thing," I said, "needs to be explained. Why is it that Whitehead, a consummate mathematician, in later years repudiated mathematics and courted the arts and poetry—things of feeling; while Santayana, a consummate poet, in maturity repudiated poetry and fell into the arms of physics? It's a twentieth century phenomenon."

"One reason is that Santayana wasn't a consummate poet!" he laughed.

"Now, now!"

"Oh, yes. My friends advised me to stop writing such old-fashioned stuff."

"One never learns the truth from friends. Only your enemies tell you that."

"At the time I had no enemies. They came later. And I shouldn't exactly call them enemies . . . Oh, yes. The verse was a mistake. So was a great part of REASON IN SOCIETY. In my latest book (DOMINATIONS AND POWERS) I don't separate art, science, and the rest as I did then. I call them 'elements' of society. You can see in this book what I should have done in THE LIFE OF REASON. It was there, but I didn't do it . . . THE LIFE OF REASON was too derivative. I hadn't read much. I did devour the REVUE DES DEUX MONDES. It's conservative, but so was I. They ran a number of travel stories—but none so good as this one on Tibet. (*The book by Maraini*.) I had been reading Hegel—the PHAE-NOMONOLOGIE DES GEISTES—and the idea appealed to me: a history of the human spirit. Lucretius has some good things on early life—prehistory. But I wanted to treat it differently—not history as a moral from the Bible."

"That's a cartoon," I commented.

"You change truth so that it's easier to remember . . . But I didn't know enough. Now I treat all that quite differently—ideas as growing out of material events. The art of government—I suppose it is an art, though there are no artists!—(We laughed.) —consists in working *with* material forces. Oh, I suppose there are artists occasionally, like Napoleon, issuing the Code, calling himself a son of the Revolution, and restoring the monarchy. But government has to be confined to material things—and mili-tary—if you are ever to have a world order. The spiritual things should be left to separate elements. You can't force a culture."

"Somewhere," I said, "perhaps in PROPOSED ROADS TO FREE-DOM, Russell says that he knows of no better aim of a state than to promote the material well-being of its citizens. When it attempts anything else the result is a failure.

"That's it exactly!"

"Then the newspapers have reported you accurately, for once."

"Scribners has an effusion department." (He laughed.)

"Effusion or infusion?"

"Where you diffuse yourself! They sent me a questionnaire with twelve questions, hoping I would answer one. I answered two—it was four or five pages—and sent it to them, saying they could print it in whole or in part. Maybe it has got around . . . I distinguish between demands and needs. If a reformer wants his reform to be propagated naturally . . ."

"The generative order of nature?"

"Yes—he has to serve a real need, not a demand. There's a difference between propagation and propaganda. I detest dogmatism, in politics or the Church. It's the missionary side of the Church I object to. Religion, like everything else, should grow out of the nature of the people, not be forced on them when they don't want it."

"A salesman has been defined," I said, "as a person who sells you something you don't want for money you haven't got." I continued, "A few days ago you said that the life of the mind has to be institutionalized in order to prevail. I gather that you aren't interested in prevailing."

"I don't want to prevail as an institution," said Santayana firmly. "I mention that at the end of the book. If people adopted the system I advocate, they would soon rebel. The young people and romantics who don't like order would rebel—because, you see, it's a rational system. In a little parable at the end I make that clear. Otherwise it would be dogmatic. And I'm not offering a choice: either my system or another."

He picked up Pound's letter again, while I glanced at my watch.

"The book—the reviewer's copy," he said, "should be here soon." He was evidently referring to DOMINATIONS AND POWERS. Reverting to Pound, he asked, "Do you suppose he's got it?"

"No," I said. "Judging from the letter, he wants it and thinks the publishers are holding it up."

"He thinks there isn't enough honey—what does Lucretious say?—honey on the rim of the cup filled with—what do they make absinthe from?"

"Wormwood."

"Yes, wormwood."

"There isn't a drop of wormwood in all your writing."

"Well, a lot of people feel differently."

(He looked down, and I thought how long and Spanish his head seemed today, as if painted by El Greco. There was a knock on the door.)

"*Avanti!*"

(A Sister opened it partially, then closed it quickly.)

"It must have been for someone else. They often make that mistake, or was it my tea?"

I rose to go. "I don't want to tire you," I said.

"You're not," he replied. "People come to see me later, after tea."

"I think you should rest a little before they arrive."

"I'm expecting another young man from the States," he said "His name is Coolidge. Mrs. Toy wrote me to expect him."

"Mrs. Toy who owned that portrait of you?"

"That was a mistake! The portrait belonged to Mrs. Parkman—a friend of Susana's. Mrs. Toy had a photograph of it. I didn't see the proof of the frontispiece in the TRITON edition, otherwise it wouldn't have appeared as it did. The original is in Rome here now, in the Andreas Anderson museum."

He offered me his hand.

"Don't you think I should give you a vacation?" I asked.

"As you wish. I suppose your days in Rome are numbered."

"I leave the twenty-seventh."

"Ah, well, then it isn't immediate."

"If, however, I don't tire you, I'll come tomorrow."

"I have nothing to do."

"Well, then, *au revoir.*"

I took my leave.

MARCH 20, 1951

The Colosseum! For how many years has it been a tourist-trap? For how many centuries has it served as a rendezvous for rogues? Here Cellini boasted of having raised the Devil—more literally than usual. Not that I encountered any devils . . . For days, I myself had passed there unmolested by any menace whatsoever—but my time had arrived.

Nearing the Colosseum today I was accosted by a young man with a pimply face. He spoke in broken English. "I am a Portuguese sailor," he said. "Can you direct me to a steam-ship office?" I assured him that I was also a stranger, and he went his way. An incident of no importance—except retrospectively.

I had barely knocked on Santayana's door when I heard a loud "*Avanti!*" Santayana was standing in the middle of the room. He came forward and shook my hand.

"I've been out taking snapshots in the neighborhood," I explained, holding up a camera. "Today I didn't bring you any puzzles." He sat down in front of the left window.

"I have a confession to make," he said simply.

"Confession," I commented tritely," is good for the soul."

"We got that thing you brought yesterday all tangled up," said Santayana. "I was showing it to the Sister and telling her how they use them in sick-rooms."

"Children like them especially," I said. "My friend even has one in Helsinki, Finland."

"Would you try to unwind it? It wouldn't move for us."

I disentangled the string easily and held it up before him.

"Oh, now I see! It has separate motions. Is it something flying?"

"No. It's simply abstract shape and motion. The motive is a little like leaves, but it has some perfectly round pieces, so it's not meant to be literal. Musicians like them, because musicians are used to abstract design."

"Is it an Aeolian harp? It should play!"

"Well, my friend was actually thinking of a harp one time. But, not being able to decide whether it should play or not, he grew confused and gave it up. These go very well with modern architecture, too, where you have big areas unrelieved by orna-ment. This gives a focus of interest. It is supposed to cast shadows. As I said, you enjoy it as you would a bough swinging in the breeze. Nowadays, you even find people with modern houses going out and finding an interesting piece of driftwood and hanging it up like this."

"Why don't you hang it from the electric fixture, so that I can show it to my friends?" The fixture hung in the middle of the room and was the only available support—the ceiling being twenty feet high at least. "Don't hang it so low that I bump my head, that's the only thing."

I secured the mobile.

"Can you see it?" I asked.

"Perfectly—that is I see the spots moving, but not the wires —only now it has stopped."

"You have to have a breeze."

"Generally there are all kinds of air-currents in this room." I sat down before him.

"You may tell your friend it is now hanging in my room."

"It will make him happy to hear that. You called it a toy yesterday. Well, in a sense all art—all enjoyment—is a toy for adults, but I find it charming. He is having an exhibition in San Antonio right now. There are more impressive pieces of colored plastic—some of fish going in and out of marine vegetation."

"Like goldfish in a bowl?"

"Yes,—and one mobile of his, which I have seen, represents sea gulls flying."

With interest that did not seem feigned, Santayana watched the mobile a while. I felt that one of two things had happened. Either, in a kindly way, he had decided to make amends for his reception of this novelty, which was rather brusque yesterday; or else, thinking it over, his aesthetic interest had been aroused. After all, he once nearly became an architect. His interest in the mobile's motion was almost child-like in its eagerness.

"Usually," he said, "there's plenty of air. This room was reconstructed." He explained numerous alterations that had been made in the clinic. "This one wall here is almost entirely of wood, you see. After supper, I used to take a little walk in the garden. When I came back I could see light through big cracks in the wall, and in the room across the way. People here don't always sleep with the windows open," he laughed, "but they get the air anyway."

End of paragraph, I noted mentally. One of the charming traits of the sage, I thought, was that his punch-line, so to speak, ends on a merry note. The laughing philosopher!

"I hope the pictures I took of *San Stefano Rotondo* turn out well," I remarked. "I even got *La Navicella*."

"In America they'll think it's a gas-tank," Santayana warned.

"A gas-tank?"

"Yes, it's so round." I realized then that he was talking about the round church, *San Stefano*, not the reproduced Roman boat made into a fountain.

"Once a year (though it's dying out)" he continued, "they have a fair in front of *San Stefano*. It honors the saint. I think it's the day after Christmas, and a very ancient thing."

"In San Antonio," I countered, "we have medieval mystery plays still performed before the mission." I told him how the Franciscan friars had composed *Los Pastores* in the old days of Spanish rule to bring the Gospel story to the unlettered Indians.

"I've seen tableaux around here like that," said Santayana, "but they don't move. You just have different pictures. The Sisters here always set up a little stable at Christmas, with the Christ-child and the wise men—*Los Reyes*, the Spaniards call them. Only here, the child is over-size. It's a modern doll. The Sisters have sewed a little chemise for it. But the other figures are more historical—not in costume, you understand—I mean they're more old-fashioned."

I asked him if he had ever seen the carved *santos* of the American Southwest.

"I've never been to the Southwest! Oh, I've seen the canyon —what is it?"

"The Grand Canyon."

"The river?"

"The Colorado."

I mentioned how touching is the pious art of ignorant people, and yet how, in a sense, all sacred art necessarily falls short of its object and to that extent borders on the grotesque. He agreed.

"We had such tableaux in Avila, I remember."

"If they hadn't had that landslide," I said, "I intended to take some walks around there, as you describe them in PERSONS AND PLACES."

"A friend of mine did that," said Santayana. "He wrote me that he found it much as I had written about it. He even went to *Sonsóles*."

"I wanted to go there."

"Well, he reported it was still as I had said, only there has been one change. In addition to the model ship hung up in the shrine, giving thanks for a miracle, there is now an airplane." We laughed. "Someone's life," he said, "was saved in an airplane, so it's there now with the seventeenth century ship."

"The age of miracles isn't over," I said.

"Apparently not."

"The good Lord still has some vitality left in him."

"Oh, we *know* that," Santayana laughed roguishly.

I felt we were playing our duet pretty well today. I recognized the punch-line and changed the subject.

"One thing I've been wondering," I said, "was how you found this place."

"I knew about it all the time. There are two chapters in Florence—in fact, it's all over the world. Strong bought some land just below the Blue Nuns in Fiesole. He built a villa—oh, a small one—but it was near them." He explained some details of how the land was acquired. "I used to take walks around there," he said, "but I didn't like it very much. It was too hilly —but you got glimpses of the valley below. That was beautiful. I liked Cortina better for walks. It's level."

"Level?" I asked. "In the Dolomites?"

"Cortina is in a valley; it has mountains on all sides." He described how small and scattered Cortina had been when he first went there—until it became a resort and ski-ing center. Also the Germanic—rather Austrian—character: Cortina having been turned over to Italy after the first war. Santayana liked a modern steeple built next to an old church there—not a *campanile*, but a separate steeple. It was the landmark of the village.

"I was adventurous then," he said, "and used to walk uphill quite a way—of course not really very far. I don't like to walk uphill on the way back."

He described the houses.

"There is no agriculture," he said, "only grazing. The barn is right next to the house. The animals are a furnace. In winter it gets very cold up there, but in summer you never see any animals. Oh, I saw a few on my walks, but most of them are up in the mountains with the shepherds. I noticed how the mountains go up with you as you climb. They don't get smaller. There's a natural explanation, of course, but it's a paradox." He smiled inquiringly.

"I've just been re-reading your chapter on travels," I said. "It seems you were disappointed in Greece."

"Yes," he replied. "I had bad luck with my guide—an orange merchant. He didn't sell oranges on the street, you understand, but he was a merchant. We didn't see all the place. He did teach me a little modern Greek poetry—I tried to pick up some modern Greek to help me with the classical language."

Here Santayana began quoting in Greek, but had to stop.

"It gets away from me now," he said, "but the subject is 'The Kiss': 'I loved her when she was ten years old . . .'"

We laughed.

" 'But I have never forgotten that kiss,'—oh, there's more to it, but I can't remember it."

We commented briefly on the Mohammedan custom of child marriage.

"I don't see how you remember as much as you do," I said.

"Why, I learned it by heart."

"I've learned things by heart too, but I can't recall them now."

"Then there was another poem," he went on, "about an Island the Turks destroyed. You don't destroy an island, of course, but the people on it. 'Now' " he quoted, " 'only Glory walks over Aspis—and this is a wreath woven from the few herbs which remain—blackened herbs.' "

"That's really very sad," I remarked.

"I don't know exactly," he said, "where Aspis is—it's one of the smaller islands."

"In travelling," I said, "you recommend that the traveller have a fixed station in life—definition—before he travels. I've been wondering how far one can go in that. Probably Russia has solved the racial minority problem better than the United States."

"In the United States," he said, "they all want to be assimilated."

"Russia respects the local cultures," I said, "though it's more theory than practice."

"They speak their own language—but they say the same thing," said Santayana. "It's like the Church." We laughed.

"Well, how far can that really go? We've had a lot of experience lately with racial prejudice—the master-race, and so forth."

"Yes, the Germans—Fichte, for instance—think that angels live at the North Pole. The devils live near the Equator. Most Europeans," he grinned, "are a bastard mixture." I thought we had ended a paragraph on a merry note, but more was to come.

"My brother Robert who never knew anything . . ."

"Oh," I protested, "he probably knew what everybody else knew."

"No," said Santayana, with a twinkle in his eye, "he knew everything everybody shouldn't know—well, my brother Robert used to say that at Genesis we were all niggers. But when Cain killed Abel and the Lord said, 'Where is your brother?' Cain was so scared he turned white!" (Laughter.)

I then told him the Mexican tale, which he had apparently never heard, of the Creation. The Lord had taken some clay, molded it, and placed it in an oven to bake. He set Gabriel to watch the oven, and instructed him to remove the cake when done. Gabriel dozed, with the result that when he took it out, the cake was burnt black. That was the origin of the black man.

Somewhat irritated, the Lord molded another cake, saying, "Now, Gabriel, I want you to watch this carefully, and don't burn it!" Gabriel watched anxiously—so anxiously that, when he drew forth the cake, it was underdone. That was the origin of the white man. Completely out of patience, the Lord molded a third cake and said, "Gabriel, this is your last chance. Either you get this right, or else!" Gabriel took his stop-watch and thermometer and went to work. At precisely the right moment he drew forth the cake. It was a golden brown. Origin of the brown man—most perfect of God's creatures!

"Yes," Santayana mused, "every race has its own angels, even black."

"Have you heard of that popular song in Spanish," I asked "called *Angelitos Negros?*"

He had not. I told him its substance and he seemed touched.

"Well," I continued, "but is there a cosmopolitan type developing? Suppose there are forces at work making a man at home wherever he goes in the world?"

"I knew a Rothschild like that," said Santayana. "He was a French Rothschild. I met him in London. He seemed just as much at home in English as in German or French. But that grew out of his position. It must be an exception. And then he was a Jew."

"Ludwig Lewissohn," I said, "has just written a book on the Jews. He takes a very traditional stand. He wants them to go back to the old orthodoxy of the synagogue."

"The Jews—having been driven from their home—are by their very position international. Now you have the two schools, depending on whether you're an American first or a Jew first. Didn't I tell you my story about Jacob's dream?"

"Jacob's ladder? No."

"It must have been the other man who came to see me. You know, Jacob dreamt he saw the angels climbing up and down the ladder. He knew that must be the way to Heaven, so when he woke, he said, 'Lord, if you give me what I ask, I shall give you back one-tenth, and call you God' ".

"He was striking a bargain."

"Yes, but notice: Lord means master. If he provides, 'I will call you God.' You worship what provides for you. And the story is that he had gone to sleep and laid his head on a stone. After his vision, he set the stone upright—it mustn't have been very big—anointed it and called it 'Bethel'—that means the house of the Lord. It's that stone they put later, I think, in the Tabernacle."

I protested that the Tabernacle was empty.

"Later. But when they brought out the Ark of the Covenant," said Santayana, "I think the stone was in it. There's more truth in these legends than we probably realize—even in Homer."

"Toynbee says there's a great deal of history in Homer."

"There had to be. People who listened were practical-minded. They had to think the story was true. Of course, people love stories and will believe anything."

I mentioned how the Chinese respect stray scraps of paper. Santayana responded with the story of his father, told in PERSONS AND PLACES, who would say: "It's not my opinion. I saw it written in *letras de molde*."

"The Mohammedans worship a stone," said Santayana, reverting to the previous topic, "—probably an aerolith."

"A meteorite? The Kaaba looks too big to be a meteorite. It's a huge black cube."

"Oh, the stone's inside. That's the building."

We argued about details of this, and decided we didn't actually know what the Kaaba was. I asked him if he had heard the story of the Virgin Mary and her trial by water. He hadn't, so I told him.

An apocryphal manuscript declares that Mary was the youngest of a large family. To preserve her pure and undefiled, the family sent her to be educated by the priests—the Jewish equivalent of a convent education. But when she reached puberty, "lest she defile the temple," a guardian was appointed. The guardian was Joseph, a widower. Shortly thereafter, Mary became pregnant. Joseph naturally fell under suspicion. The two were subjected to the Ordeal by Water. This consisted of administering to the suspects a cup of "bitter water" with which was mixed dust from the Tabernacle floor. If the suspect became sick from the draught, he was judged guilty; if he emerged healthy, he was innocent. Both Mary and Joseph drank the drink, and emerged unscathed.

"That's not Catholic," Santayana commented. I agreed that it was apocryphal.

"I saw a fourteenth century mystery play once," he said, "where Joseph is told about Mary's pregnancy. Someone had seen an angel in the neighborhood. 'Then,' says Joseph, 'I wished I had been beguiled!' " (We laughed) "Of course, in the end everything was made all right, but Joseph's sentiments were natural."

The time, I noticed, was flying, so I drew out a card.

"As usual, I have some questions," I said. "I have hesitated to ask you this . . ."

"Very well," he put in.

". . . but it applies to all the people I'm writing about— the revenues of intellectuals. Would you ever have been able to live off the income of your writing alone?"

"Oh, no!" he replied. "I never tried to.* I might have, as a newspaper man. I was going to teach—but if that didn't turn out, I was going to study architecture. My appointment at Harvard was only temporary, you know."

Here he retold the story as it is found in PERSONS AND PLACES.

"As my writing grew better known, especially after I lived in Europe, I was able to afford little luxuries, but then my income increased from other sources."

He explained that his mother turned over $500 a year from her Spanish widow's pension to him. She had left him $20,000 after her death, which, at 5 per cent made $1000 a year. The pension, of course, stopped when she died. There had been
*Cp. Richard Butler, "Well-financed by his prodigious writings, he remained a self-exile in Europe." *Memories of Santayana,* THE COMMONWEAL, Vol. LVII, No. 3, Oct. 24, 1952, pp. 57-59.

a period of hard times for the family: the panic of '73. Russell Sturgis of London had been prevailed upon at that time to settle 100 pounds ($500) a year on her for life. A big problem had been one Beacon Street house. Two others, told about in PERSONS AND PLACES, were usually rented. When the Beacon Street house was sold times got better.

I asked if this was the house in THE LAST PURITAN. "No," he answered, "it was the good one where a bachelor uncle of mine lived by himself."

"You haven't seen the MS of PERSONS AND PLACES," he mused. "There is some material left out about mad relatives and friends. Our uncle was amiably mad—but every family had one. The Grews asked me not to tell about one in their family—a really sad case."

"New Englanders always had a lunatic chained in the attic," I remarked satirically.

"Even Russell Sturgis, when he grew old, lost his wits. He was with Baring. The government had to come to their assistance. They nearly failed. I think it was Russell's mind." Santayana tapped his forehead significantly.

"Is the firm still in existence?" I asked, surprised.

"Oh, yes . . . I knew one son: Cyril Baring. He was in the Army, and he had a friend, Geoffrey Stuart. I call them just A and B in PERSONS AND PLACES."

He recounted the story as told there. I listened intently, because, on the basis of this story, one speaker on the radio forum, "Invitation to Learning" had guessed that Santayana never possessed a friend in his life. The objectionable part of PERSONS AND PLACES had related how Santayana, meeting one of these young men after a number of years, would have nothing to do with him. The explanation? "He had lost his good looks." Finishing the story and the episode at the Bank of England, Santayana said, "I can see Fleet Street now, as I walked down it that night."

There followed the exegesis of the offensive story that I was waiting for. "I met him (*Stuart*) later, you know, crossing the channel. He looked bad—he had been in India, I think, and was probably bored to death."

I suggested that alcohol might have helped. We discussed alcohol and regular Army life.

"No," Santayana decided, "it probably wasn't drink—just boredom. I didn't see much of him on the steamer. I was afraid of getting sick. I went upstairs where there was air. I only saw him a moment afterward."

Santayana's vivacity showed this was a crucial episode, but whether he knew my sleuthing interest in it was hard to tell.

"Memories, memories, memories," he sighed. "I've told you almost all I know. Most of them are in my book."

"Oh, no!" I protested. "You have told me a great deal more and I don't regret coming. Round the work of the most articulate writer there is a penumbra."

"Indeed? Well, the memories I haven't told are mainly unpleasant—but I have no secrets."

No, I thought, not for one who can tell a hawk from a hand-saw when the wind is southerly!

I checked with him then on his name when he played leading lady in a *Hasty Pudding* show. The title was *Lady Papillonetta*.

"It ran in 1886," he said. "There was another, where I played Maid Marion in *Robin Hood*, for the *Institute*. That was in '84. The *Institute* was called the *Institute of* 1770. I don't know why they picked me."

"You were probably good-looking."

"I knew women. Our family always used the same sitting-room, Spanish style, and I was with Susana and my mother constantly. I was also small—not really small, but the other boys were taller. Have you seen that picture?"

He rose, and took out a LIFE clipping from a volume of PERSONS AND PLACES. "I wasn't made up," he explained, "so I don't look very feminine." He also commented on the photograph in the frontispiece. It had lost, he thought, through reproduction.

I prepared to go. I explained that tomorrow I should not see him. I had to buy rosaries for some American friends, and didn't want to postpone the shopping trip till the last minute. My private reason, in addition, was that Santayana needed a rest from my interviews.

"Saturday night," he suggested, "you might like to go up to St. Peter's. The Pope is restoring an old service to its proper place. It used to be on Saturday morning. This is more appropriate. It's the vigil before the Resurrection. It starts at ten, and ends at midnight. Then the mass begins. You needn't stay for the whole thing, of course, unless you wish." I thanked him for the suggestion.

"The only mass I ever attended when a Pope officiated was conducted by the one they just beatified—Pius X. I was sitting on a bench between two priests on one side who were talking a language I didn't understand, and a Roman priest on the other. That is the only time I heard people making themselves understood to each other in Latin. The Roman priest asked them in Latin, 'What nation are you?' '*Slavoni*' they answered. Later he said to them: '*Cantant epistolas in lingua greca.*' (They sing the Epistles in Greek.)" Santayana seemed amused at the Latin Church having its liturgy talk back to it in Greek.

I mentioned again that I had to shop for rosaries tomorrow. They must even be blessed by the Pope! Santayana remarked, "They do that in quantity."

"Mass-production!" I exclaimed, and took my leave.

MARCH 21, 1951

"If you want to profit by your short stay and see as much local colour as possible," Santayana had written me before I arrived in Rome, "I should suggest the *Hôtel d'Angleterre* . . . The numerous restaurants are crowded and good; you can easily pick up the necessary Italian, and learn what category and what dishes suit you best. My favourites for every day, when I lived in the town, were the *Roma*, the *San Carlo*, and the

Fagiano."

The night I arrived at the hotel suggested by Santayana, the meter of the taxi read: L.120. I asked the driver, "*Quanto?*" He replied, "One dollar." This was a fine bargain for him. The exchange stood at no less than L.650 to one dollar! Having changed no money as yet, I paid.

The first night, the clerk gave me a double room, No. 20. Thereafter I occupied No. 49, a single. It was a corner room, boasting two windows. Furnishings consisted of a day-bed, a desk, a wardrobe, a chest of drawers with a fine, heavy, carved and gilded mirror suspended over it, and a fire-place adorned with a pen-and-ink drawing, very operatic, showing an incident from the Roman Empire: "*Le Donne Germane si uccidono con li loro figli, per non rendersi prigioniere dei Romani.*" (German women committing suicide, along with their sons, so as not to fall prisoners of the Romans.)

This incident was one, apparently, wherein the sons had been very little consulted. Their mothers had up and stabbed them! The inscription concluded:

"*Regno di Tiberio*
Pinnelli inv. e inc.   Roma 1829"

A sop to the visiting Nazis of a few years ago?—I wondered. The drawing, however, seemed to have hung there a long time.

White and blue were the prevailing colors of the room. Great stiff lace curtains covered the windows, which made deep bays—the walls being very thick. I could close the shutters at night if I so desired. On sunny days, the room provided the cheeriest of spots for me to transcribe my notes—the German women committing suicide over the mantel notwithstanding.

This room possessed no bath—only a wash-stand in a separate entrance-hall. Opposite, however, was a bath-room. This had to be opened ceremoniously by the maid or houseboy brandishing a key big enough for a castle. The water must then be drawn, and two fine towels—suitable for a hippopotamus —must be laid out neatly. The tub, also designed apparently for Primo Carnera, is the only tub I have ever been able to lie down in and twiddle my toes: in the universe of tubs a paragon.

In still another room lurked the water-closet of the kind Santayana had agreed: Possession is nine points of the law. A remarkable contraption, when all is said and done! This work of ceramic art was adorned—inside and out—with blue crysanthemums!

The elevator displayed a will and personality of its own. It was an ancient bird-cage affair of wrought-iron. Often it stopped at my floor and refused to budge higher. The procedure was then to ride to the bottom and try again. This failing, a universal practice was to howl down the well, "*Ascensore!*" in the hope that some handy-man might materialize and set things to rights. This seldom happened. Like most guests, rather than wait, I preferred to walk *down*—only using the lift to save breath climbing up.

As you descended the stair, you could study a marble tablet commemorating some monarch's visit—a King of Spain, I think —at the hotel.

I must not omit a further distinction of the elevator. For the ladies, it had little mirrors inside, and a plush seat for those who might grow faint during their perilous ascent.

In this bird-cage I met the nymphomaniac. I use the term in no derogatory sense. If the good Lord had not intended some people to be women, French, pretty and passionate, I doubt if He would have felt any compulsion to create them. In any case, I met her the morning of the sixteenth when the manager was showing me an assortment of single rooms. "Where," I asked the manager by way of precaution, "is the bath?"

At this juncture, a slim, attractive brunette with the coiffure of a Zulu burst from her room, crying. "*Je veux changer ma chambre!*" Noticing me, she continued to the manager emphatically in good English, "I told you *yesterday* I wanted my room changed!" The manager assured her something would be done. The Zulu retreated to her doorway, where she struck a provocative pose, as if to say: "*I* am Tandaleo!"

"Where," I meanwhile repeated, "does one take a bath?"

"He can use *my* tub," The Zulu trilled in dead-pan, mock-seriousness.

The manager hustled me down the hall, and the nympho-maniac—for the nonce—was seen no more. Eventually she took a room directly over mine . . .

A commotion at the room-clerk's desk attracted my attention one evening around six. The crew of an American B-29 (I judged) had just arrived. There, in the midst of the clamor, the tall, blue uniforms, and the flight-bags cluttering the tiny lobby, the Zulu was fluttering.

I entered the elevator. Two flight-officers stepped in, and on their heels, the Zulu.

"Where are you flying from Rome?" she asked them.

"Marseilles," a captain announced—indiscreetly, I thought—but were we then at war?

"Oh," gasped the Zulu dramatically, "you simply *must* take me along! I *must* get to Marseilles at once."

The officers grinned. The bird-cage reached my floor.

"*My* room," the Zulu murmured, "is on the *next* floor."

"So's ours," the officers chimed in as one man.

"You two must come to my room with me," she translated freely from Mae West. "I want to talk to you about Marseilles."

With leers of pleasure, the officers answered, "Okay, lady," and the cage disappeared, carrying aloft its wild, wild bird.

Later that evening the crew, much flushed, seemed to have found liquid refreshment at the bar. In their midst sat the Zulu drinking, fluttering and chattering excitedly.

Again I boarded the elevator. The Zulu and one or two of the crew joined me. As we rose heavenward, she flourished a scented handkerchief and exclaimed, "Oh, I have had such *dreadful* news today!" The flyers looked boozily sympathetic. As I left the elevator she was confiding to them, "I simply *must* get to Marseilles!"

The nymphomaniac's wish may or may not have been gratified. That night, at any rate, she seemed to be flying high in the room overhead. It sounded as if she and various other bodies were flying through the air with the greatest of ease, making periodically what seemed scarcely three-point landings. I gathered that, by an odd coincidence, the entire crew had found its way to the Zulu's room and spent the night there.

Such commotion was exceptional. The *Albergo d'Inghilterra* is a sedate hotel, and decent. So quiet was it that for many nights I was deceived, as I lay awake, by what sounded like rain. Every night and all night, it appeared, rain fell over Rome. (Winter had indeed been unusually wet and cold, leaving vegetation this March, a brilliant emerald green.) But it was not rain that caused that steady sound. It was the plashing of an ancient fountain next to the hotel. Had the place been rowdy, a fountain's murmur would have been lost in the hubbub.

The effort to reconstruct my dialogues with Santayana required, I found, almost eight hours of concentration daily. It was remarkable, in itself, that they should have been dialogues. Most old people simply deliver monologues *Ex Cathedra*. By evening, as I lay in bed, I was haunted by the fear that I had forgotten something. Also, I feared that unless I set down the dialogue of the day at once, intact, it would merge with prior or subsequent talks—as has actually taken place in my mind now, a month's distance away. In general, the reconstructions succeeded—but scraps of talk, sometimes important, would get lost, then pop up later, out of context, during my midnight meditations.

Thus, at some time, Santayana had said he knew Whitehead—had been in the same room with him, and had heard the words attributed in OBITER SCRIPTA to a "famous mathematician." Whitehead had said: "There are some questions that can be answered, but they are unimportant; others are important, but they can't be answered." This, and a good deal besides, not very flattering to Whitehead, was related also in Part III of PERSONS AND PLACES, which I copied; it was omitted from the present edition of MY HOST THE WORLD.

Santayana had known Housman—I recalled—: had sat next to him at dinner. This, he said, was before he had read the

Shropshire Lad.

At Cambridge or Oxford, again, he had met Salvador Madariaga. I praised his recent Rise and Fall of the Spanish-American Empire.

"When I knew him," said Santayana, "he didn't think much of Spain."

"Oh," I objected, "this history is very sympathetic."

"An apology?" asked Santayana with, I thought, some contempt. That was all I could recapture of that conversation.

Strange street-sounds, at night, sometimes held my attention. A certain whirr baffled me. It was as if an airplane were flying low at intervals of fifteen minutes. I located the source of the sound finally, by day. It was an electric bus. It buzzed regularly along the neighboring *Via dei Condotti*. Then, one night—years after the hit had swept the United States—I heard someone whistling "*Nature Boy*" . . .

Santayana had advised purchasing a map, and I had obtained one. With its aid I found my way around easily. I was happy not to circulate this time as a green tourist. It was not incumbent on me to pay my respects to every famous shrine that I had visited twenty-four years earlier. Yet, by varying my walk from the hotel to *Santo Stefano* each day, I saw all that I could remember and much besides that was new.

Trinità dei Monti was located a few blocks from the hotel —an exquisite stage-set. Not far away gushed the Fountain of Trevi. Nearing the fountain one night, I passed the façade of an old church. There, in the darkness, on the stone platform in front, three couples of adolescent boys were dancing. In the doorway of the church sat one more, playing the mouth-harmonica. Can a people with such gaiety in its blood, I wondered, ever perish?

Occasionally, day-time apparitions surprised me along the *Via dei Fori Imperiali*. They were only "characters," materializing from nowhere, suddenly obsequious at one's elbow, offering fountain-pens, watches, or other trinkets from the black market. I never knew where they came from, being always abstracted as I walked or entranced by some vista. They lounged along tourist-lane, waiting. Then, like a flash, but always polite and speaking intelligible English, they appeared—ghosts in broad daylight.

"Can I show you round the city?" a youth asked me one cloudy day. I was strolling past the Victor Emmanuel monument, toward the Colosseum.

"No, thank you," I replied—noticing simultaneously his good English and his face pocked with acne.

"Couldn't I be of some service to you?" he insisted. I realized then what he was insinuating, and repeated, "No thanks—not today." As I left him he called, "I'm here every day, if you need me."

I couldn't use him, but I wondered how many soldiers had.

On the morning of the twenty-first—the day I had told Santayana I was going shopping—I awoke late. This time the dripping fountain seemed an augur of rain. The sky was heavily overcast. I set out, taking along my trench-coat.

At the corner of the *Via Bocca di Leone* and the *Via dei Condotti*, in an art store I had passed many times, I noticed a black-and-white sketch of a Renaissance courtyard. That, I decided, might make a gift for someone in the States but, for the time being, it could wait. I turned right, and was soon at the *Piazza di Spagna* and antique dealers' row. Nothing interested me along this street particularly. I did drop in on an exhibition of modern painting—mainly of women, half-nude, with long, pendulous breasts. Critics in Roman newspapers had perhaps panned the exhibit. The painter was discussing some clippings with a group of his friends. He looked disgusted. The exhibit was in fact mediocre and I soon left. Rosaries, I knew, would be sold in the neighborhood of St. Peter's. I continued in the direction of the Tiber.

The Tiber, as usual, was muddy. I noticed a large boat, painted blue, tied up in front of the Castle of San Angelo. It advertised bathing facilities. Does anyone swim in the Tiber?' I wondered, or do they take mud-baths? In the distance loomed St. Peter's, no longer obscured by slums. The *Via della Conciliazione* made a magnificent approach.

A large, new building to my left caught my eye. It was the headquarters for the American Catholic Action. It was also, I noticed, a club for service-men. In a window religious articles were displayed. It was not they, however, that attracted me. I was hungry. I gathered that meals were served inside. The lunchroom was empty, but soon two girls, one white and one colored, came in and ordered a slim breakfast. They were obviously travelling on a shoestring and counting their pennies. It pleased me that, close to the Vatican, at least, no color-line existed—and in an American club!

After breakfast, I inspected the rosaries on view there. The store itself would not be open till one. Meanwhile, I thought I might revisit St. Peter's. As I walked up towards the basilica, I passed countless stores selling religious wares, but the director of the U.S.O. had already referred me to the best store, he said, in Rome—near the Pantheon, so I hesitated to buy. St. Peter's itself left me cold.

Emerging from St. Peter's, I consulted my map, then directed my steps along the Tiber and toward the Pantheon. In the distance, huge black clouds were gathering. Lightning flashed. The Castle of San Angelo and other buildings nearby stood out boldly in the bright sunlight against the livid clouds. Wind began to blow.

I reached the Pantheon in a cloudburst. Through the hole in the dome, rain poured down hundreds of feet, splashing hard on the marble pavement below. All round stood the dark altars—once shrines of Olympian gods, now tombs of kings and queens, with Christ or the Virgin presiding over them. I went out and sat at the foot of a pillar. Tourists scurried in and out—one, alighting with her chauffeur, not even bothering to extinguish her cigarette as she entered the temple. Several bus-loads, looking like American school-teachers, inspected the place. But the language they spoke was not English. I failed to recognize it—perhaps it was Slavic. Styles, I inferred, are becoming international. Every youth in Rome seems to own a trench-coat. The movies: universal solvent.

When the down-pour changed to a drizzle, I sought out the religious shop. The walls were lined with all the paraphernalia of piety: figurines, reliquaries, pictures, crucifixes . . . I chose a little wooden, carved cherub (a request), picked out four rosaries, then decided to buy two bronze crucifixes—one for myself and one I hoped my best friend would accept. As she wrapped the packages, the clerk presented me with a St. Christopher medal of great beauty. Now my plane, on the way home, could never crash!

Only after I had left the shop some blocks behind did I remember: the rosaries had not been blessed! Here was a problem of conscience. How would my Catholic friends know whether the Holy Father had made passes over their rosaries or not? I could tell them he had, and they would be forever secure in their illusions. Or I could simply fail to mention the oversight. I trudged on, not feeling quite right about it.

I reached the *Corso*. It amused me to hear one lad whistling "*La Raspa*"—so far away from Mexico. I walked down toward the Victor Emmanuel monument, looking for leather-goods. I found none worth purchasing. I did run across a little brass coffee-pot, suitable for brewing *caffé expresso*. This I bought for myself.

Retracing my steps, I stopped in at a little bar near the hotel. Roman "bars" are wonderful: tiny, clean, glittering with liqueurs, offering tempting sandwiches, together with black coffee or chocolate for teetotalers.

Indeed, all Rome—like Madrid—had been astonishingly neat and clean. On mentioning this later to American friends, they would reply, with true national egotism, "Of course! It's for the American tourists." One, however, guessed what is perhaps nearer the truth: universal poverty. Not a scrap of paper or a stick of wood but somebody in Italy or Spain can make use of it. Be this as it may, the two capitals were cleaner—even to the side-streets—than any American city I have seen lately. I refuse to believe that all the reasons for this are negative. Italians and Spaniards like their monumental cities spotless—

At Arles

where a picture of the Crucifixion
hung in the museum above a bust
of Antinöus.

I see thy likeness in all beauteous things
So much are beauty and thy likeness one,
Thee in the painted death of Mary's Son,
Thee in the marble loves of pagan kings.
Each day, each hour, its drop of trouble brings
To swell the flood of sorrows long since done
Till down earth's cheek the loosened waters run,
Darkly foregathered in her frozen springs.
What wealth of tears were this, to weep today
When he's a god, who was Antinöus?
Why mourn for Jesus? Christ remains to us.
Cruel Perfection! Every lure is thine,
Ours every grief, till Love shall pass away
That made us wretched all and thee divine.

1895   G. Santayana.

Manuscript of a sonnet by Santayana, "At Arles"

Via Santo Stefano Rotondo, 6
Rome. October 22, 1950

Dear Mr. Lind

You have written an astonishingly
penetrating sketch of me and my philosophy,
the most sympathetic I have yet seen. You seem
to know all my books and a good deal about
my life, and your proposed final volume with
me for a nucleus will be excellent. Naturally
where you have no first hand account to go on
you let your sympathetic imagination fill in the
picture, as people must writing biographies, even
autobiographies. But you may get further facts
and limits from other studies of my works which
have appeared. Howgate is accurate about facts
up to the date of his books which I had read in proof
but he has not, to my knowledge, kept up with the
rest; and he is fair about style, etc., but not
very intelligent _in excelsis_. I notice in your article
two small slips in details. I was born on Dec 16
1863, not 4; and my friend's title was Earl Russell, not of, since this is also his family surname; and he did not remain always as open
tive and trustful a friend as he was in the
first years. This is described in the third part
of "Persons & Places", not yet published. You
also over emphasize a little my attachment
to Spain. It is largely theoretical. It was
Greece and England - one also theoretical
and the other fragmentary - that were in my
mind when I wrote the "Life of Reason".
I have just received a thick volume entitled
"La Pensée de George Santayana en Amérique"
by Joaquin Durou; Librairie Nizet, Paris. A sec

Portion of Santayana's first letter to the author.

July 18, 1952

Dear Lind
    I have read this twice and find
it Splendid. My eyes are getting
weak and uncertain, so that both
reading and writing are difficult.
On my first reading I thought perhaps you repeated your classif cation
too much, and that "Intellectuals" was
vague. But I felt this less on the second
reading; also missed altogether
a quotation that I meant to ask
you to leave out, although I did
not understand it. This makes
me think that the difference of
"aesthetic" views between us is
only a difference in taste in some

Portion of Santayana's last letter to the author.

Hotel Bristol, Rome
June 10, 1939

Dear Mr. Auslander

I send you a relic for your shrine. It is an old sonnet never published; it has been re-touched, but still may represent the "ideals and aspirations" of some of us in the 1890's. I should hesitate to offer it, if you did not seem to regret those less "darkened" times. They were enlightened, but they were decadent. Perhaps the world may be approaching some new era of faith, not so wistful but more normal.

Yours sincerely

G. Santayana

Letter from Santayana to Joseph Auslander

"Through an open archway in the ruins of an aqueduct."
Entrance to the Clinic of the Blue Sisters, Rome.

"The respectable entrance to the grounds of this establishment."
Clinic of the Blue Sisters, Rome.

"A broad shady street leads gently up hill."
Via Claudia, Rome

"To the *Navicella*, a marble Roman fountain (reproduced)."
Church of Santo Stefano Rotondo, Rome,

"It's very small—but it looks like a decent church."
The Parish Church of San Marcos, Madrid.

"Those look like little stunted trees in a square in the foreground."

"No, that's a donkey."

The Parish Church of San Marcos, Madrid.

with or without tourists!

I drank my *caffé negro* and consumed several sandwiches, then paused in front of the little art-store again. That Renaissance courtyard looked more inviting than ever. I went in, and asked to inspect some prints. I emerged with the courtyard sketch, and a number of red crayon drawings by Del Sarto.

The rain had resumed, so I returned to the hotel. There I took out my purchases and examined them with some satisfaction. I set one bronze crucifix on my desk, where it remained throughout my stay in Rome, with its solemn inscription from St. Ignatius of Antioch: *Amor Meus Cruci-Fixus Est*. The Renaissance courtyard sketch I placed on the mantel over the fireplace, hiding the suicidal German women. The Del Sarto drawings I distributed over the chest of drawers. All in all, I felt that my mission had been a success. I could return to Santayana free from the worry of not finding what I wanted at the last minute and so disappointing my friends.

Also, I decided to have the rosaries blessed.

MARCH 22, 1951: Maundy Thursday

As I opened the door, Santayana was resting on his chaise-longue, his feet covered with a blanket. On his lap I recognized the German work about Alexander the Great which he had mentioned previously. On the table beside him lay an anthology of modern poetry. Later, I noticed that he had been reading in it some verse by Robert Lowell.

"Aren't you cold?" I inquired.

"No. I haven't moved from this spot, and the window's open. But I haven't any appetite. I didn't eat any lunch."

"Trying to reduce?"

"No—not exactly. Life," he grinned, "isn't rational."

We laughed at this. I took off my coat and sat down next to him.

"I've had an adventure!" I said.

Passing the Colosseum, I had been accosted again, this time

by a character in a tan coat who identified himself also as a Portuguese sailor, hailing from Brazil, who knew a little English. "Can you tell me the way to a steamship office?" he asked. This time I indicated the center of town vaguely, and explained that I was a stranger. He then proceeded to explain that he had to leave town quickly. At this juncture a pedestrian passed us. The "Sailor" intercepted him. The man talked no English, being Italian. My Italian was negligible. "Will you translate for me?" the Sailor requested. "*Parlez-vous français?*" asked the Italian. "*Un petit peu,*" I rejoined.

That single phrase constituted me a dragoman forthwith. The Sailor desired me to interpret for him. He could show this Italian, if he wished, some valuable bolts of men's suiting which he kept in a jeep. We were walking, as I endeavored laboriously to interpret, toward the Convent on the Caelius. Nearing a café, the Italian suggested that we might more conveniently transact our business there. *Bien.* The Sailor disappeared and returned shortly with three bolts of suiting, each, as he stated, containing six and one-half yards of cloth.

Perfunctorily the Italian examined the goods. "*C'est bon,*" he decided. He had meanwhile identified himself, by passport picture and certificate, as a student of economics in the University of Rome. Economics was indeed his interest! The two bargained for a while, finally reaching an agreement on price. The Italian took out his wallet, and produced half the desired amount. The Portuguese exclaimed: "But I need dollars!" He was leaving town. I suggested that he change the money at a bank. "The bank," he objected, "won't be open till three. I must leave by two." Then the Italian made an ingenious suggestion. Why couldn't I accompany them to his home, where he would pick up the rest of the money (in Lire), change it for the Portuguese into dollars, and so do two gentlemen a great favor? I said I carried no such amount with me. Besides, I was on my way to a hospital and was late already. After some further attempts at persuasion they gave up the attempt. I, meanwhile, finished my coffee. The student of economics

paid the bill. I left. It had finally dawned on me that the two
were partners in this game.

"That's not what I'd call an adventure," Santayana commented.

"Well, for me it was. I got a cup of coffee out of it."

"Then you cheated *them*," he laughed.

I could see he enjoyed my gay mood. Perhaps it cheered
him in his indisposition. I told him how I was having the beads
blessed, after all, for my Catholic friends.

"How do you know," he asked archly, "that they're really
being blessed?"

"I don't."

"Perhaps the Holy Ghost runs along unknown channels!"

A moment later, more seriously, I told him of visiting St.
Peter's and finding it as devotional as the Grand Central Station.

"It's too lordly," I said, "too wordly, too elaborate. I
think it's vulgar."

"It is," Santayana agreed. "I used to go there occasionally,
and I found it so. But one afternoon I walked over in the
late afternoon. The sun was coming in through the west window,
in the apse."

"Where the dove is."

"Also in the side chapels the light fell horizontally. I never
felt the vault so, previously. You looked up through shafts of
light. That gave me a different impression. Then, of course, it's
meant for spectacle. Saturday night it will be very different."

"I was only seventeen when I visited here last," I said. "The
visual memory has remained intact, but I recall no mood.
However, I noticed changes on the outside. That *Via della
Concilazione* is a great improvement. You used to look out
from St. Peter's over slums."

"There were two little streets," Santayana concurred, "leading to St. Peter's. You were either too far away or so close
you couldn't see the dome in proper proportion. You could
always see it from across the Tiber. That was a standard view in
old drawings by—oh, what is the fellow's name? No matter!"

"Michelangelo didn't intend the dome to be dwarfed by the façade."

"Michelangelo didn't do it! Except the dome. He planned a square church, in proportion to the dome, with four little domes at the corners. There are two now. No: later on they wanted it to be like the old basilica—with a long nave. When they put up benches, and seat 40,000 people you'll see the difference."

We discussed changes in American architecture and culture. Santayana hadn't heard of Frank Lloyd Wright, so I promised to send him some pictures of his work.

"In any case," I said, harking back to the previous subject, "the new approach is magnificent."

"One of the last times I walked to St. Peter's," Santayana observed, "I went with the tallest man I have ever seen. He said he was six feet seven. That doesn't seem possible. But the King used to have guards you would see on the street, and they may have been that tall. This man wrote me a letter which pleased me very much. He's from Austin, Texas. I told him, if he were in Europe, to come see me. His name is Richard Lyon—Richard Sea-Lion," Santayana laughed. "I called him Dick. When he came to Rome, he knocked at the door. When I opened, I wasn't sure if the door would be high enough to admit him. 'I forgot to write you,' he said, 'how tall I was.' "

"Is he a teacher at the University?"

"A student. He was twenty-two or three then. He must be twenty-five now. He was hoping to get a scholarship to Oxford."

"A Rhodes scholarship?"

"Yes, but he's too old. They can't be over twenty-five. He wanted, I think, to become a priest, but couldn't quite bring himself to it. The thing that pleased me so much was what he said about one of my books. 'The one I like best,' he wrote, 'is DIALOGUES IN LIMBO.' And what dialogue do you think he liked best?"

"AVICENNA?"

"No. Normal Madness! That was remarkable, a young man hitting the bull's eye with the first shot."

"Dialogues in Limbo is your favorite, isn't it?" I asked.

"Yes."

"My favorite in that is The Secret of Aristotle."

"Oh, well, that's more difficult. But for a young person to pick Normal Madness was remarkable."

"Has anybody ever compared you to Aristotle?"

"Why, I'm a student of his—but I don't claim to be like him. I follow his physics, but not his belief that categories of thought control nature. That was fanciful and naïve. The Greeks thought *their* ideas were the only ones."

"And since nobody in Greece taught Greek . . ."

"Well, there were a few foreign teachers. Herodotus must have known Egyptian, unless he always went around with a guide. But that was the exception."

"I have come to consider it a great privilege," I said, "to know the Plato and Aristotle of modern times—Whitehead and yourself. You emphasize difference, distinction—in the Aristotelean manner. Whitehead was a Platonist, laying stress on unity."

"I don't think you'll find much of Plato in Whitehead," Santayana objected.

"Oh, yes! He was always talking about the *Timaeus*."

"But that's the least Platonic of the dialogues. I don't know it well. It's very complex, a cosmology. Plato borrowed things from Heraclitus."

"Well, those, I suppose, are the opposite poles: adequacy and consistency."

"Yes. But people who are always after unity live in a world of their own making, a world of ideas."

"A dream-world?"

"Yes. Adequacy is difficult. All animal thought is a fiction. It doesn't necessarily represent the reality underneath. It only points to something. Of course, there is a reality underlying any given essence—but the essence isn't the reality."

"You speak of fictions," I said. "Still, that leaves open the question of whether the fiction is true or false."

"Any essence is true for the mind at the moment. But it is not necessarily indicative of the material reality underneath —which may be very different."

"That brings me to a question," I said. "When you say 'matter,' you don't seem to mean Newtonian mechanism."

"Newton has nothing to do with it. And I don't mean Descartes' notion of matter as extension. Extension is a mental category. It's all around, of course, and there it is. (We laughed). But I don't see how Descartes gets any division in matter, if it is just extension. It doesn't take care of radiation either."

"No," I agreed. "Where you have radiation you have a field, in which radiation is everywhere at the same time, or could be. I wonder if, when you use the word, matter, you aren't adopting the word of your adversaries and refuting them with it. Your 'matter' reminds me of Plato's 'matrix' as it appears in the TIMAEUS."

"It is infinite potentiality of real existence. It's useless, of course, to define a real thing. You can call it matter, or motion, but it can't be defined. Yet without it nothing real would happen."

"This is the place for intuition?"

"Yes."

"Aristotle," he continued, "borrowed from Democritus, who saw the whole process—except that he imagined that these atoms had unchangeable geometric shapes. There have to be vortices. He found it more intelligible to make them in squares and triangles and regular shapes. I don't follow him there. Any shape is possible. To imagine otherwise is to indulge in poetry—or literary psychology.

"As such, there's a great deal to be learned from literary psychology. One mind can guess what is in another mind— almost identically. So long as you stay in the human sphere you're safe—because you're talking about minds made in more or less the same way. The danger is when you extend that method to the sub or super-human sphere."

"Then," I said, "you have anthropomorphic projection."

"Yes. Now, in the DIALOGUES IN LIMBO I make Democritus say things he never said—but he could have said them. Then, in PHILOSOPHERS AT COURT, I change the history a little."

"PHILOSOPHERS AT COURT? Is that published? I never ran into it!"

"Oh, no. It's an unpublished play, about Plato at the court of Syracuse. It's blank verse. I even did a play called *The Marriage of Venus*—it's a defense of free love." Santayana chuckled.

"Why don't you publish them?"

"Oh, they might give people the wrong idea. People would say, for instance, that I didn't understand Plato—that I wasn't serious."

"I think you should publish them anyway. When did you write them?"

"PHILOSOPHERS AT COURT—I think I did it some time after my travels, around 1910. THE MARRIAGE OF VENUS goes back almost to my undergraduate days. I did all my best poetry then, you know. The first twenty sonnets—except the first two, which I wrote to introduce them. I thought of calling the play THE MARRIAGE OF APHRODITE, but I changed it to Venus because the Latin words go better in English. Wedd* suggested some names to me for PHILOSOPHERS AT COURT. I worked on it at King's college. He gave me the use of his room for the early part of the summer. I read Petronius there. I hadn't heard of him before. I liked one story in particular—about a widow whose husband died. She was so grief-stricken that she went to live near his tomb. This wasn't far from where people were crucified. They used to post guards there at night, so that relatives of criminals wouldn't come and take the bodies away. One of these soldiers made friends with the widow. She took a liking to him, and he began to spend the night with her. Then one night a body was missing—relatives had noticed the absence of the guard, and had carried it away. The guard became frightened and asked the widow's friendly

*Nathanial Wedd, a teacher at Cambridge University.

advice. 'Why don't you take my husband's body?' she said, 'and put it up there?' " Santayana quoted La Fontaine's ending for this story, in French.

"How can you remember so much?" I asked. "Do you have a visual imagination: do you see the page?"

"No, I hear it."

We laughed heartily at Petronius' story.

"It reminds me of Murger's tale about THE MAUSOLEUM," I said, and gave a synopsis.

"The same story, imitated," was Santayana's comment.

"What is PHILOSOPHERS AT COURT about?"

"Well, Plato went to Syracuse three times, but I combine the trips. Dionysus had been his pupil. Now he was to govern Syracuse—at least for a short time. So Plato was going to reform the government."

"Didn't he have everybody running around doing geometry?"

"All sorts of things that didn't work. He couldn't even keep Dionysus' friendship—of course, now he was an older man. But Dionysus knew what could be done and what couldn't—the same idea as in my book just coming out . . . Then I have Aristippus in it. Dionysus says Aristippus must leave because Plato is coming. There are also three courtesans. They are told that the court is going to reform. The courtesans go to meet Plato as he comes off the boat. One of them, a matron, tells Plato about all the nice songs and dances the other girls know. They tell him how handsome they think he is. He says where he comes from they don't have such singing and dancing, and that there's going to be reform. As he leaves them, they say he's an ugly old man and has no sap left in him."

"You should publish that."

"Cory is going to put it in my POSTHUMOUS POEMS. I told him about it. Just the poems alone wouldn't sell—it's too slight a volume. A few people would pick it up to see what was in it, but that would be all. With the two plays included, it would make a nice volume."

"And LUCIFER? Has that been published?"

"Oh, yes—three times. I have an old edition of it, printed alone. The cover was black, but now it's badly faded—though I have given it no use. You can find LUCIFER with other things in the TRITON edition. The big libraries and universities should have it."

"That brings up some details I'd like to bother you with. I know you dislike detail, but I know you dislike inaccuracy more."

"I'm very inaccurate."

"Well, I go home from here and write down these conversations, and some things escape me. I'm not sure, from the third part of PERSONS AND PLACES, for example, just what year you travelled. Was it 1903?"

"No, it was 1905. I remember in Cairo, reading the newspapers about the Russo-Japanese war. The French were for the Russians—that surprised me, because the British and American papers were for the Japanese."

"That was on account of the Anglo-Japanese naval treaty."

"Was that in effect then?"

"Yes—even some years earlier. And the Russians and French had an entente."

"To keep the Germans off."

"That led to complications. When the President of France and the Tzar of Russia met on ship-board, the band played *The Marseillaise*. The words are pretty rough on people like the Tzar."

Santayana began to quote from the *Marseillaise* in French. "Most of it," he argued, "is harmless. Besides, bands don't usually sing."

I smiled at his perspicuity.

"Another question," I went on. "What did you say that other bag was, beside the Gladstone?"

"A 'kit bag.' It's the older one." Santayana explained how, if a person was not too tall, he could fold trousers and coat on the bottom and they would not need to be pressed when removed.

"Who was it," I said again, "that left spirit out of account, in the genesis of matter?"

"Do you mean Anaxagoras?" asked Santayana.

"Yes, that was the one!"

"He had this idea: that like can only generate like. If a flint and stone make a spark, the spark was already there—only very small! You see, he was confusing essence with matter. The scholastics also say that like generates like—only it must be on the same level of dignity. A man can generate a man, but not a monkey. And a monkey can never be anything but a monkey."

We laughed. I thereupon asked permission to transcribe Pound's letter. I assured him it was not to be published.

"That's all right," said Santayana. "And you can publish anything I say or write you—but I don't want the third part of PERSONS AND PLACES to appear before my death. In general I have taken care not to tell people any secrets I don't want them to know."

I kept my own counsel at this point, but I knew that we both knew what he meant. I transcribed the letter exactly. (See above, p. 65f.) Then I requested the text for the "ATOMS OF LIGHT" quotation.

"I can quote you the whole verse: it's only a quatrain," said Santayana. He did.

> *Blow what winds would, the ancient truth was mine;*
> *And friendship mellowed in the flush of wine;*
> *And heavenly laughter, shaking from its wings*
> *Atoms of light and tears for mortal things.*

"That is exquisite," I commented. Then: "What was the name of that island we were talking about the other day: Aspis?"

"Rhodes!" he cried. "I thought of it after you left. How silly of me to forget."*

*It was PSARA. Information furnished by C. A. Triantaphyllakos of the Royal Greek Embassy.

I then obtained Duron's address at the Ministry of Instruction in Paris. Santayana estimated he was now a man in his
fifties, also that the second part of his book would not appear
soon. Duron, he believed, had once considered entering the
priesthood. "I hope he reads my new book," said Santayana.
"He will be better informed if he does." The two were friends,
but had not met for some years—the last time being in Glion,
Switzerland.

I checked on the themes Santayana had said were in his
mind when he wrote the Last Puritan: friendship, marriage and
—was it the mixture of cultures?

"Oh, not then. That comes later, in this meeting of East and
West in Hawaii."

"Religion?"

"The Last Puritan is a religious theme, isn't it?"

"I was trying to remember which you said."

"Yes—marriage. Of course, people have asked why I never
married. I never cared particularly for women . . . Codman asked
me about marriage—but that had a special background. He meant
marrying an American woman. I couldn't do that. I didn't want
a family divided as mine was."

"Didn't your life as an intellectual have a bearing on it?
Domesticity doesn't mix well with the life of the mind."

"That was the principal factor—a clerical one. I had chosen
a clerical life almost from the beginning, and that ruled out
marriage."

"The first day I came," I said, "when I stated I wanted to
write your biography, you asked, 'Where will you get the
facts?' Now that you know what I intend—not a definitive biography, but a study relating your ideas to history and society—
your criticism and creative work in it—do you think that
Persons and Places is enough?"

"Yes. Of course, some day someone will look up all the
sources and print everything about me—they always do; but
it won't be important. I have no secrets . . . Actually, I don't
know a lot about my background. Someone calls me the 'pillage

of Europe.' "*

"Pilgrimage?"

"No, pillage. Naturally, I had a European background. The universities in my time were all classical, and English and German."

"Colonial."

"Yes ... Then, I only *mention* certain people in Persons and Places: Cory, for instance. Then there was a man, Roberts, that I travelled with, after Christ College. We travelled up the Rhone together. Westenholz, (the German baron) introduced us, I think, in England in 1910. We travelled together in 1912. He was then twenty-five. In Cologne we had what you would call an 'adventure.' We went to see the 11,000 virgins at St. Ursula's— you know, their skulls."

"Guaranteed virgins?"

"Martyrs—there they were, the wall papered with their skulls. Only an old fellow there said that the manuscript describing them was smudged. Where tradition read 11,000, he said it was 11 M—which could be *milites*: soldiers. Where it reads *virgo* or *virginae*, it might be the name of their captain. So that eleven soldiers and their captain became 11,000 female saints."

"Did that destroy your devotion?" I asked.

"I didn't have any," he chuckled.

"One more detail," I proceeded. "Do you like bull-fights?"

Santayana said he liked *Spanish* bull-fights. I offered to send him The Brave Bulls, illustrated by the author, Tom Lea.

"I don't know anything about Mexican bull-fights," he said. "I suppose they're quite different."

"Oh, no. They're the same." I explained how *matadores* travelled back and forth between Spain and Mexico.

"Have they changed it about the horses?" he asked. "They were often gored in Spain."

I said they were padded now, even in Spain.

"That must change it," he observed.

"No," I replied, "the *picador* works as usual. He maddens
*Lewis Mumford.

the bull, and also weakens the neck muscle." (Sidney Franklin, I think, denies that this is the purpose.)

"Then he can't throw a man so easily?" Santayana queried. "I've seen horses thrown, but not very high."

Santayana, thinking I had in mind a book of pictures, said I had better not send it—he would only have to store it in the next room.

"Before I go, one last question: Is the 'genteel tradition,' as you conceive it, an American specialty—a combination of religion and watered-down aristocratic breeding?"

"It could exist in North Germany," Santayana smiled. "You remember Irma Schlote's family in THE LAST PURITAN?"

"Yes."

"Mrs. Alden, Oliver's mother, is another example. She was very refined—and still pretty practical."

"Bourgeois? She made a marriage of convenience."

"Yes. And she knew a lot—as they do in girls' schools. Of course she really didn't know anything."

"Have you seen Grant Wood's picture: *Daughters of the American Revolution?* It's printed in THE MEETING OF EAST AND WEST."

"Wood? Is he well known?"

"Yes."

"That must be the man who painted my portrait—that gross one I told you about. I don't remember his first name."

"Grant Wood's stuff is very slick."

"Oh, then, this must be another man. Would you like to see a photograph of the portrait?" He got up and took a post-card photograph from the dresser drawer. It was not a likeness, and by no means the sensual or diabolical thing I had inferred from his description. I felt it was incompetent, and more or less said so. The inscription on the back was the truest part of it: "The greatest man I ever painted"—(signed) Harry Wood. I said I liked Lipinsky's portrait much better.

"He came out with some Italian photographers," Santayana remembered. "They took many poses, and Lipinsky made one sketch of me standing to greet them. Then he went home and picked the photograph he liked." We were unable to decide whether it was charcoal, pencil, or grease-pencil. (Later, I read on the back of the portrait itself: "Charcoal drawing.")

I prepared to leave.

"You're coming tomorrow?" asked Santayana.

"I should like to."

"At the usual time, then. Mr. and Mrs. Cory are visiting me later."

I offered to stay away if I interfered. He assured me I would not if I came at two. I left him seated in front of his dresser drawer, holding some photographs.

As I walked home it occurred to me that the mobile had disappeared!

Also, I found on entering the hotel that my notebook was gone. Had I left it with my conspirators of the afternoon—the Portuguese "sailor" and his accomplice—or was it in Santayana's cell? If so, it had my real name in it, with the San Antonio address: not Bruno Lind!

MARCH 23, 1951: Good Friday

"*Avanti!*"

Santayana was seated by his left window in the arm-chair, his feet wrapped in a blanket.

"You are having guests later," I explained, "so I came early."

"Oh, they won't be here till five," he answered, "but it's good for you to come early. We can talk."

"Here are the snap-shots," I said. "The photostats of your portrait won't be ready till tomorrow."

"Not Monday?" he inquired. "Monday's considered a holiday and you won't be able to get it. When are you leaving?"

"Tuesday, at six."

"In the morning?"

"No, evening."

"Well, then you can get it."

"I have had good luck with things so far—obtaining them on time. Besides, the place is just round the corner from the hotel."

I handed him the snap-shots.

"That's number 69, *Ancha de San Bernardo*," I said, "but it doesn't look like your birthplace as you described it."

"The one here on the edge, or the one in the middle?"

"The middle."

"Oh, I'm sure that's a modern building." He covered the top with his finger. "I was only there once, as a boy. My father said, 'There's where you were born.' It only had four storeys."

"They might have added to it," I suggested, "but it looked pretty modern. The next two pictures are the parish church of *San Marcos*."

"I don't remember it. I was too small to remember."

"While being baptised?" I joked.

"It's very small—but it looks like a decent church."

"It's small and round inside. It has a dome."

"Yes, I see."

"This picture shows the steeple."

"You mean the *lantern*."

"Yes."

"Those look like little stunted trees in a square in the foreground."

"No, that's a donkey!" (The donkey's silhouette in the foreground was actually not very plain.)

"Oh, I see now."

I showed him a snap-shot of the church of *Monserrat*, which I had first mistaken for *San Marcos*.

"The Virgin," Santayana mused, "worshipped as of Monserrat. That's a famous convent in Catalonia."

We looked next at pictures of *San Stefano Rotondo*.

"It looks much bigger than it is," he observed. Seeing the *Navicella* in dark silhouette, he exclaimed, "They'll think it's black!" Then he told how the reproduction of the fountain had been made, with pieces of the old Roman boat inserted.

I next showed him a picture of the entrance to the Convent of Blue Nuns.

"Ah, now that's nice!" He examined it with his magnifying glass.

The following snapshot was a closer view of the clinic.

"It looks very large and solemn," he said.

The next, even a closer view, brought the comment: "This looks even larger."

"And solemner?"

"No."

Color snapshots which I had taken, but which were to be developed in the states, ought to turn out well, I told him. The palm tree in front of the clinic was in bloom. Big orange spikes hung down against blue shadows. He liked the idea, but would accept no snap-shots when I offered them. They would obviously accumulate in a room well littered already.

"I never explored Madrid," said Santayana. "I was always passing through. I would stay with Mercedes Escaleras. And I was never free, that is, alone, to really see things. If I went sight-seeing it was usually to the museum or to the bull-fights." Santayana did not recall the present bull-ring, which is Moorish in architectural style. It was perhaps built after his time. It had looked new to me.

On leaving Madrid, I told him, the airport bus had encountered a procession out of the Arabian Nights. The bus, a two-decker with plastic top, enabled one to see far down the street: as I recall, the *Avenida de José Antonio*. There, coming toward us, I saw four golden carriages with plumed horses and liveried footmen attired as of the Eighteenth Century. Behind followed a troop of sixty *spahis*, Moroccan cavalry with capes and turbans. From each turban protruded a silver spike.

"Undoubtedly an ambassador," said Santayana, "presenting his credentials."

Passengers on the bus, I recalled, had said it was the British ambassador, but I had seen no British flag. Others guessed it was the opening of the *Cortes*.

"In PERSONS AND PLACES," I said, "you speak of the 'spiritual regeneration' of the *Falange*, and of your nephew being killed in the civil war. What is the *Falange* like in Spain?"

"It's religious, with political and military elements."

"Is it representative of the middle classes?"

"Everybody in Spain is more or less middle class. No, there were even some nobles in the *Falange*. It's a kind of Fascism."

"Then it isn't the Italian or German kind, which was a front for the bourgeoisie."

"No. It's more religious. Even Mussolini made an agreement with the Church. And they had trouble in Italy with the scouts. The Church wanted Catholic scouts, so they had two movements. Mussolini united them, so they would all know they were Catholic. It doesn't amount to much. Perhaps they all go to communion once a year . . . And Franco intends to restore the monarchy—but not right now." Santayana laughed. "He likes the job himself, but he's training a boy."

"What is the boy's name?"

"It must be Alfonso."

"He was only twelve," Santayana continued, "when they sent him to Spain, and of course they had to give him up." Here followed a long dynastic discussion of Bourbons and Carlists. "Jaime," said Santayana, "is in more direct line than the boy, but he was deaf and dumb. They say now, though, that he's cured. He married into the Carlist branch, and so he unites the two lines and has the best claim to the throne. And of course, they're all devout," he said, with a twinkle in his eye. "Even Isabella was devout—though she is supposed to have had many lovers."

"Ugly as she was?"

"But she was very sympathetic—*simpática*." Here he retold his sister Susana's escapade in the royal park, as related in PERSONS AND PLACES.

"*Se ha enamorado de mi*," Santayana quoted with evident relish. "Susana in those times was very attractive. I was only on the way at the time, but I was told about it. My mother didn't go walking because of her pregnancy. But even later, Susana was considered to be very unusual. She wasn't, but I have continued the myth. She was unlucky."

We returned to the subject of Queen Isabella. "Piety once saved her life," said Santayana. "A mad monk stabbed her, but she was wearing a medal."

"Of St. Christopher, no doubt."

"I don't know. It was very large, and then it might have been the whale-bone corset, not the medal."

"Another myth?"

"Very possibly. Her corset was transmuted into a religious medal—by a miracle." We laughed over this, as usual.

Santayana mentioned that he was expecting Robert Lowell any time now, and was memorizing some of his poetry. He knew some of it by heart already. When I said he must have it perfect for his arrival, he exclaimed, "Oh, I'm working on it!" He alluded again to Lowell's remarkable vocabulary. He was much intrigued by one line of Lowell's. "The Lord survives the rainbow of His will." "I don't know what it means," he said. "I only have a theory." This theory brought in Ahab and the white whale from MOBY DICK. God had created man out of the slime, but also other creatures. Man was fated to kill them and be killed himself in turn. That multitude was the rainbow. He then quoted from an elegy of Lowell's for a friend dead at sea, somewhat in the mood of his own elegy to Warwick Potter dead under similar circumstances:

> . . . *"Ask for no Orphean lute*
> *To pluck life back. The guns of the steeled fleet*
> *Recoil and then repeat*
> *The hoarse salute."*

"I could almost have written that," said Santayana, "only I wasn't good enough."

Alexander the Great, about whose reign Santayana was now reading, became our next topic of conversation. "Are you going to do an essay on him?" I asked.

"I may never get to it."

"Oh, yes you will!"

"Well, perhaps. This book (*a German text*) and Tarn are about all I shall read on the subject.

"Have you seen Harold Lamb's book?"

Santayana had not. I explained that Lamb had ignored what others had said about Alexander, had read the sources, and had retraced Alexander's travels. Santayana seemed interested.

We compared the Greek city-states with the squabbling United Nations. "The trouble is," said Santayana, "that they're all equal. Unification is usually imposed by a foreigner."

He showed me the two-volume work by W. W. Tarn: ALEXANDER THE GREAT. A big volume was the critique of sources. The little one (how scholarly!) was the LIFE. I took down the title of the German text: GESCHICHTE ALEXANDERS DES GROSSEN, by J. G. Droysen. "This book," he said, "contains the only known authentic portrait of Alexander." We discussed the possibility of coins carrying it. I mentioned Rostovzeff's specialty in coins. Then Santayana showed me a set of historical plays by Helen Bartlett, including one on Alexander. "This has another photograph of a statue of him, full-length," he explained, "but he's wearing a Roman helmet. Alexander wore one like Brunnhilde's, with two eagles on it. What I like about this statue is the hands—: they're soldiers' hands. He used to throw his spear a great distance. When he was in battle he would carry a spear for offense and then, if he lost his spear, he used his sword and shield for defense." Santayana leafed through the other plays, including one on Napoleon. "This woman," he said—referring to Helen Bartlett—"thinks she is an intellectual. Actually she's a dilettante." We compared Napoleon and Alexander. I said Alexander was probably the greater. He had enjoyed a princely education.

"But it wasn't much in those times," Santayana argued. "Napoleon knew much more."

"Well, Alexander had Aristotle as a tutor."

"When he was thirteen! All he seems to have remembered

were some mistakes about the Caspian Sea."

Fleetingly I remembered Santayana's own play: PHIL-OSOPHERS AT COURT. There, truly, philosophers had figured as supernumeraries.

I then asked if he had seen my lost note-book. He had not, but invited me to look for it. It was nowhere to be found. I remained Bruno Lind.

"It must have fallen into the hands of those rogues of yesterday," I decided. The character, I told Santayana, who had been in such a hurry to leave Rome by two o'clock was back at his old post near the Colosseum. I had glimpsed him, complete with tan overcoat, pushing a stalled car—*not* a jeep!

In the third part of PERSONS AND PLACES Santayana refers to being "stranded in England" from 1914 to 1919. I now inquired about this.

"I was stranded only because I didn't want to go home," he admitted. "I had a return ticket, but I didn't use it. I was undecided what to do. My friendship with Russell was cooling. I went back and forth from London to Paris." (This could only have been after the Armistice.) "That," he recalled with some warmth, "was when I met my friend, Stuart. Russell was always very kind and hospitable. And the arrangement wasn't just friendship, (he grinned) but economy. I paid for my meals and ate out a great deal, but still it had been a saving. Once, at Cambridge, Russell had invited me to stay, and let me make use of his rooms, but he was having dinner with Lionel Johnson. I wasn't invited. He preferred eating alone with Johnson. I tell about Johnson, you know. He was a Fenian—a political Irishman. He was Welsh! He said it made no difference. They were Celts. I never went with Russell or him to their haunts. Johnson finally always bolted the door—he thought he was being followed."

"When did Russell die—was it in 1933?"

"It must have been before that," Santayana thought. He recalled being in England for the lecture on Locke in 1932. "Comedy after tragedy!" he sighed. Russell had died before that. I said I could look it up.

Next I inquired if there were anything in particular that I should know about his publishing history.

Santayana had been dissatisfied with the early format of THE SENSE OF BEAUTY as it had come out of Scribners—too compressed and academic.

"They have always listed me under *Education*," he laughed. "Even now, when they send me yearly accounts, I'm under *Education*."

After THE LIFE OF REASON, Scribners did not publish Santayana for a long time. It was Constable, and—"a trope within a trope, a circle within a circle"—Dent, who did WINDS OF DOCTRINE and EGOTISM IN GERMAN PHILOSOPHY. Logan Pearsall Smith had engineered Constable's editions. Santayana had met Mr. Dent at Harvard, when Dent was visiting there. The publisher had proposed that Santayana write an introduction to a new edition of Plotinus. Santayana said he didn't know enough about him, but would do an introduction for an edition of Spinoza.

We returned to the topic of Russell. I asked about the bigamy trial, at which Santayana (I thought) had testified.

"Oh, no! That was ten years later," said Santayana. "I testified at the libel trial. Those sisters who were daughters of Russell's nurse libelled him, and he sued. I really don't know if there was a seduction. The reason I testified was that I was with him that time on the yacht. You remember: We went down the Rhone and the Saone and the Seine. I was with him when the seduction was supposed to have taken place—not all the time—(and it wouldn't have taken long!) It was after this trial that Russell paid me a great compliment. 'The judge could see you were a gentleman,' he said."

"And a gentleman," I laughed, "can do no wrong!"

Santayana, I felt, didn't care for this quip, but he only remarked, "My education, he meant, hadn't been accidental."

"Did that trial have any repercussions for you in the States?" I asked.

"Some papers printed it," he replied, "but they mixed me up with a Russian named Komchov. He also travelled with Russell on the yacht—but that was earlier. Komchov was dead at this time.

"You know," he continued, "there's an expurgated and an unexpurgated edition of that story. The English publisher, at the last minute, decided that it (PERSONS AND PLACES) might be libellous. I don't know if the two sisters I said may have been Russell's mistresses are still alive. If they are they're over eighty."

"They should feel complimented if they read of it now," I laughed.

"No doubt. But if they thought they could get an indemnity —what's the other word?"

"Damages?"

"Yes, damages, then they might sue."

"Is the American edition expurgated?"

"No. There was no danger there. But they had to paste in a few pages in the English edition . . . There was a lot more Russell told me which I didn't write about."

The talk drifted to Harvard. Trumbull Stickney had been instrumental in having Santayana's first book published. "He was a classicist," said Santayana. "He knew Plato." I chuckled and asked, "Are you damning with faint praise?"

Evidently he was not. He simply meant that Stickney was a professor of Greek who knew his subject. Then he retold the story of Stickney's ostracism by some Harvard snobs, because he had used the word, "gorgeous." I remarked that such a word would not put him beyond the pale there today.

"Divine?" Santayana queried.

"Well, yes. 'Divine' would ostracise him," I admitted.

I said the place was turning into a factory—that Harvard had the best that money could buy—but money couldn't buy everything. Santayana thought Conant was a mistake—too narrow a specialist. Lowell was better, but his hobby was the houses (*i.e.* dormitories).

We digressed to Hutchins of Chicago and his restoration

of the classics. Santayana didn't recognize the name, so I gave a short account of Hutchins and told several anecdotes.

"The name (*Hutchins*) doesn't sound very classical," Santayana observed.

As for the Harvard houses, Santayana said that during the war several had had to be closed. I remarked that they were lavish and expensive.

"When a thing is good it becomes expensive," said Santayana. "Then only the rich can have it. I don't see any disadvantage in that."

Not, I thought to myself, when you live off your mother's inheritance! But this quirk of his was well known to me, and I did not argue.

Santayana reminisced about the Delphic club, of which a 1950 journal lay on his book-shelf. "Lowell's houses," he said, "have had a bad effect on clubs. They were never eating-clubs exactly, but you ate together often. Now I think you have to take most meals at the houses." He recalled that the cryptic initials: *D.E.C.* had meant "Daily Exercise Club," but also "Drunks' Exercise Club." Santayana had found this club "thoroughly delightful."

We returned to publishing history, but I picked up only a few details, such as objections to print, paper, etc. So I asked whether his sense of being personally misunderstood had influenced his interest in myth.

"That came after THE REALM OF ESSENCE," he said at first. "Before that I was understood."

I restated the question and mentioned his account of William James. "Well, James had a preconceived notion about me. But I had other friends. They knew what I was like."

In THE REALM OF ESSENCE, at the beginning of the chapter on "Implication," Santayana states that an essence is grounded *in itself* without any reference to any other. This seems to deny relationship with anything else and hence all logical implication. I inquired about this point. He agreed that at least through its *difference* an essence is related to *everything* else. No essence, in Santayana's philosophy, actually exists. Nevertheless, I thought I saw a similarity between his thought and Whitehead's system, wherein every existing event presupposes all others as a *field*.

The room was getting chilly. Santayana was beginning to cough. I remembered the guests he would have later on, so I took my leave—promising to come again tomorrow.

MARCH 24, 1951

When I opened the door, it was precisely two P.M. Santayana was sitting by the left window, with a table and tray still before him.

"You see, they haven't taken the things away," he said.

"Have you finished?" I asked.

"Oh, yes."

I handed him a bouquet of three pink roses. "So that you may have a happy Easter," I explained, "and brighten up your room."

"Thank you very much. I'll have the girl put them in a vase when she comes for the tray." I placed the roses on his desk.

"I see you have something else. Is it the pictures?"

"Yes," I said, taking off my coat. "I think they turned out very well." At this moment the maid came in.

"*Ha lei un vaso*," I requested in the only bad Italian I had used in Santayana's presence, "*per i fiore?*"

"*Si, signore*," she answered, and presently returned with a vase. We set the roses on the table next to the chaise-longue. I took out the photographs, one small and one large, of Santayana's 1896 portrait.

"These are splendid," he exclaimed, "—especially this one." He examined the larger photostat. "You are very lucky." He held it in various lights. "It reproduces almost exactly the quality of the original."

"How big is the original?"

"About this size," he said, indicating the smaller photostat.

"You see that sarcastic smirk on my lips?" he pointed out. "I was disgusted with the world at the time. When I was young I was very unworldly."

It was not a "sarcastic smirk" on his lips, but the look on his face was not what could be described as devout.

"You must have been a very solemn young man."

"Oh, I was."

"Here," I said, "is the original (*frontispiece*). I'll place it here on your desk. I want to thank you for entrusting it to me, and having confidence that it would return in good shape. You really have a great faith in human nature."

"Oh, yes—in some human nature."

"Or is it just Nature? You have faith in the material course of Nature."

"For limited periods," he laughed.

I took out the portrait of him made in 1950. "I should greatly appreciate your signing these two large ones," I said.

"I'll be glad to. The other day you didn't ask me."

"I wanted to have the other enlarged first. Also, I hesitated, because I didn't want to involve you in 'manufacturing mementoes.' "

This had been his objection to my bringing a wire-recorder to Rome, which I had hoped to use for some readings of his sonnets. He said nothing. After a pause, he asked, "Where shall I sign them?"

"Preferably on the back," I said. "I intend to use them as illustrations, and writing might spoil the composition, don't you think?"

"Anything you like." On the first he wrote: "*For Bruno Lind*—as he wrote he said, as if talking to himself: 'Oh, yes—because it's a gift.'—*Easter*, 1951, *George Santayana*." I thanked him and gave him the other. "I must write something different on this one," he chuckled. The inscription ran: "*George Santayana in 1896 and still alive in 1951.*" I put the photographs carefully in an envelope, for rain threatened outside. There had been some drizzle as I came in. Santayana was obviously feeling better today. Several times before I had noticed a kind of chemical effect, a delayed reaction, after something had pleased him. Was it the roses? Was it the youthful portrait? In any case—as it would in most people—a pleasant thought had irradiated irrelevant matters. The sage was in high spirits.

I had brought along a red crayon drawing by Del Sarto—a youth praying. The title was CARITÀ. "I thought you might like to see this," I said. "I have never found a better portrayal of devotion."

"Del Sarto!" Santayana mused. "He was once called the perfect painter. That's why Browning didn't like him. It spelt perfection, finality—decadence." Santayana laughed. "He looks afraid."

I couldn't say to whom—of the two—Browning or Del Sarto, he was most disrespectful. Luckily it didn't really matter. A comparison occurred to me which could not affect the issue one way or another.

"He reminds me of Parsifal," I said.

"Isn't his head too small?"

"That's stylistic, like Michelangelo. It makes the body gigantic." Santayana remained unconvinced. He sat looking at the portrait of himself in his youth.

"It's a glossy finish," I pointed out, "because I intend to use it as a frontispiece. The older portrait I'll put in the rear of the book. I think it is discouraging when biographies always use as a frontispiece a portrait of the man when time has done its worst—physically speaking, of course," I added quickly. "Lipinsky's portrait of you is superb."

Santayana continued to concentrate on the 1896 portrait. "Yes," he agreed, "that was when I was at my best. If I had had a choice, I should have chosen never to be born. It's so arbitrary, being anything in particular—when you could be everywhere. That is the nature of spirit, to want to be everywhere—not interested in just certain things."

"Doesn't Sophocles say that in OEDIPUS REX: 'Better than to have lived is never to have been born at all'?"

"Yes—but he got it from someone else. It goes beyond Sophocles."

" 'Next best,' I continued, 'is to have died young.' Doesn't he say that?"*

"Yes, but I don't agree with that. Once you're launched, who knows if it is better or worse to stop?"

"At any rate, a person is never around to find out."

"To persevere and persevere—that's the American motto."

In a rush of enthusiasm which later I realized cut off what might have been a solemn meditation on Death, I exclaimed, "And I have never felt so American as at this time, revisiting Rome and all the antiquity of Europe! I sympathize with mature civilizations, but I feel young. I feel the future."

"America has many opportunities. I only wish they wouldn't try to make everybody like themselves," he commented.

"The French," I remembered, "were said during the Revolution never to be more universal than when they were most French. The Americans, on the contrary, seem never to be more American than when they try to be universal."

"Ah, but the French—even under Napoleon—saw they had enough of a world at home to conquer . . . Of course Napoleon wasn't a Frenchman. He spoke Italian. And he had the Latin family feeling. He put his brothers and sisters on thrones."

"Sometimes they proved unreliable."

*Housman's winged translation runs in part as follows:

> *What man is he that yearneth*
> *For length unmeasured of days?*
> *Folly mine eye discerneth*
> *Encompassing all his ways . . .*
> *Thy portion esteem I highest,*
> *Who wast not ever begot;*
> *Thine next, being born who diest*
> *And straightway again art not.*

"It's an absurd system," said Santayana, "yet for a while it worked."

We got into a discussion about Jerome Napoleon.

"He married an American," Santayana asserted, "but I don't remember that he had a throne. Bernadotte was in Norway." We couldn't decide off-hand, but I seemed to remember that he had betrayed Napoleon. Santayana recalled that the Napoleonic King of Spain lasted only two years.

"In my time," he said, "we had Amadeo. He was overthrown in two years." Here followed a dynastic discussion, ending with Santayana's comment that a Spanish ruling house, to survive, must accept Spanish asceticism.

"Have you read any books," I asked, "or written anything I haven't seen on the ascetic ideal of life, apart from doctrinal differences?"

"There are many books," he replied, "and you will find something on this in my new book. In this book on Tibet there is a picture of a saint—he must be a saint—who has lived by himself for eight years, without much food and with no books. He seems to look well. John the Baptist was a saint, even though he couldn't be a Christian because he came before Christ."

"Is there any world religion, besides Christianity," I asked, "which makes so much of martyrdom? It seems to me other civilizations have had more respect for the spiritual life."

"The Christian church," said Santayana, "began persecuting very early. That's the side I object to: the Church Militant. You know the story of Ananias?" I had forgotten.

"The Church was communistic. You had to give all you had to the Church, then you'd receive a portion for yourself. Ananias and his wife were rich. They didn't want to do that. It is said that Ananias fell dead one day. I don't know if he was helped on that occasion or not. I have always suspected the Will of God received a little help. Oddly enough, his wife died suddenly too. So, whether it was the Will of God alone or not, it showed what the church *hoped* would happen to them. Next door here (*San Stefano*) was a slaughter-house. Murals all round portray every atrocious form of martyrdom you can imagine. St. Stephen, of course, was the first martyr."

"To me," I said, "it seems barbarous that Christ, alone of all founders of world religions, died young. The East seems to venerate age."

"It does. A saint isn't usually so highly regarded while he is young. In Eastern religions he has to be like myself, very old."

"Tomorrow when I come," I announced, "I shall bring you your halo. Do you think it will fit?"

"No, I could never wear a halo."

"Perhaps one with a couple of little horns added?"

"What would the horns be for?" he asked. "I'm not married!"

End of paragraph, I thought to myself, as I caught the merry note and we laughed together. I drew out some cards with left-over questions.

"What," I asked, "did Dent want you to write an introduction for, before you did the one on Spinoza?" Santayana didn't recall. My first notation had been Plotinus, which is perhaps correct. Whatever it was, Santayana had not been interested.

"Did Russell," I went on, "have children by any of his wives?"

"He could have had, by his first one," said Santayana, "but they separated in a few months. He told me a lot of things that aren't in the book, but no matter. If you want more details, by someone who knew him, read the book by Elizabeth."

"Vera?"

"Yes, the first part isn't like him, but the end is. She may have made some of it up. The part about his locking her out of the house at midnight doesn't sound true, but it may be. If it was, he forgot to lock the servants' entrance. She got in that way, gathered some clothes together, and walked down the hill to the village. It wasn't too bad down-hill—but at midnight! And up-hill would really have been bad."

"Was he always so interested in mechanical novelties?"

"Yes, but he wasn't good at them. Oh, he knew how to manage. He ran his yacht, and that was a risk in the Mediterranean—the yacht was so small. Russell was excellent at motoring." A short pause. During this pause I reviewed in my mind two significant scenes: one from the LAST PURITAN, where Oliver Alden is driving, and much admired for his skill by Edith; the other in part three of PERSONS AND PLACES, where it is Russell who is driving, and Santayana sitting by, admiring.

"I nearly bought a motor myself," Santayana continued. "Strong had a car, and we used to go everywhere in it— everywhere that *he* wanted. I would see some cathedral in the distance and ask to stop, but he never would stop. But I was dragged to see whatever he wanted. Strong was a good man, but he was like that. Once he said, 'You've got to see *Port Royal*—where the Jansenists lived. I didn't want to see *Port Royal*—it has no architectural interest—but he took me anyway. I got out and walked half-way toward it, then turned around. 'Very well,' I said, 'I've seen it.' "

"When the crash came in 1929, I lost half my money. But at that very moment my sister, Josefina, died and left me half of hers. There were two wills. In one, she divided her inheritance three ways: between me and Robert's two children. But there was another will, and I had the advantage (he grinned) of being on the spot when she made it. I asked her how it was to be divided. She didn't understand very well, but I showed her the two alternatives. 'Why, half should go to Robert,' she said, 'and half to you.' Robert was her full brother and I was the half-brother. She was rich. She had always lived with my mother and never went out or spent anything." Santayana laughed. "When she left me the money, it was exactly what I had lost in the crash, so I was just where I started.

"When I received the telegram of her death, I went to Strong—we were in Paris then—and said, 'I'm going to come into some money, and I'm thinking of getting a motor. What would you advise?' 'We'll have to go in one or the other, then,'

Strong said—and he didn't like someone over him. So I gave it up.

"There are many places you can reach by motor that are hard to reach by rail." He mentioned an Italian town in the mountains, built on great Etruscan fortifications. He also mentioned a resort between Venice and Trieste. "I don't like the Lido," he said. "It's over-run." He also would have visited parts of the French Riviera, if the car had been his.

"My friend, Berenson, told a story about the little town of Paola. It has a pulpit out in the street, and once a year on the Saint's day, a priest mounts it and speaks to the people about St. Francis. He tells them what a fine saint is Francis of Assisi: the stigmata and the Little Flowers and all that, 'but,'—he asks them—'is this the saint we are honoring today?' 'No!' the crowd answers, 'not he.' The priest goes on to tell about St. Francis de Sâles—the women all like him. 'Is *he* the saint?' the priest asks the crowd. 'No!' the crowd roars" —and Santayana was beginning to roar himself, with evident relish. "The priest goes on about St. Francis Xavier, how he converted the Japanese— though now they've forgotten. 'Is that the saint?' the priest asks. 'No!' roars the crowd. 'Is it St. Francis of Paola?' 'YES!' everybody answers."

"I went to Paola by rail. At the station where you get off, I asked for the hotel. 'There is no hotel, but we can give you a room upstairs,' they said. I looked at it. It had no windows. I could imagine getting in bed with a thousand future living Buddhas, so I decided to try the town. Meanwhile, I was hungry. No restaurant. So I met a woman selling eggs. I asked, 'Are they fresh?' She said, 'Yes,' so I drank them, and that was my lunch. In the town, I saw the pulpit in the street, but when I asked for an *albergo* they looked confused. Finally I found the only one. They showed me upstairs. It was one big room with rows of beds, with no sheets or pillows."

"A flop-house, we'd call it," I put in.

"I decided there would be more future living Buddhas there, so I returned to the station. I had to step over a pool near the

entrance where a horse had wasted substance, but it turned out
that the room was clean. For supper I had a meal of fish out
of tins—fairly stale."

My next question was to check on the Delphic club
initials. It was originally part of the Delta Phi fraternal order,
he explained, but they never had much to do with the national
body. Eventually, like all Greek letter societies at Harvard,
they dissolved the connection. They also called themselves the
Gas-house gang. Santayana had not belonged as an undergraduate, only later. The cryptic initials were: D.E.C.—meaning "Daily Exercise Club"—that is to say, they walked from
the dining table to the front door. Also it was the "Drunks'
Exercise Club." They drank *tea!*—after chapel. Santayana drew
out a small volume: THE ESSAYS OR COUNSELS CIVIL AND MORAL,
by Francis Bacon. It was part of a set of leading English essays
given him by Delphic Club members. On a paper pasted inside,
and engraved as follows:

> *Delta Phi Club*
> *72 Mt. Auburn St.*
> *Cambridge*

had been written:

> "To our most noble
>   President
> el illustrissimo
> Señor Ruiz de Santayana
>   y Borras—
> in celebration of his
> eight & twentieth
> birthday—
> December the Sixteenth

Signatures followed:

> D. E. C.
> Boyleston Adams Beal
> Winston Clark
> Gordon Knox Bell

Warwick Potter
R. P. Blake
Julian Codman
W. C. Forbes
Ezra Lincoln
W. S. (?) Kidder—(Not a friend, just an acquaint-
ance. Santayana wasn't sure of
the initials.)
J. L. Putnam"

As I wrote, Santayana exclaimed, "My, you're going into this deeply."

I pleaded poor memory, and solicited his help in getting the signatures right.

Warwick Potter's name struck my eye. Santayana had not mentioned him in our conversations. I said that Lowell's elegy was in a kindred mood to the one he wrote for Potter.

"He was much younger—eight years younger," said Santayana. "But Lowell's poem is about his cousin, a mature man." That was all. I think this reticence goes deep.

"Was there a period in your life," I asked, "like Baudelaire's —of Dandyism? Your description of Howard Sturgis is one of the most enjoyable in part three of PERSONS AND PLACES."

"I didn't go out much, except with the Delphic club. I was too unworldly. In London, during one of the Easter or Christmas vacations I met some gay young men. There was an Australian man from Cambridge who was fashionable and had seen more of the world than most of us. Then I met 'Pinky' Rothschild—he was a French Rothschild."

"The one we talked about the other day?"

"Yes." Santayana thought it might have occurred during a vacation which included Paris. "It was then," he said, "that I got this cold."

(A cold, I asked myself, lasting sixty years?)

"I admired his command of languages . . . Howard Sturgis had a mother complex. At Howard's we didn't actually see much aristocracy. He had three daughters of the historian,

Motley, as neighbors. They moved in the upper circles . . . If you're looking for periods in my life, you could say that the first was clerical. I was disgusted with the world, especially America. Later, I enjoyed myself in the clubs at Harvard. When I went to England, I saw an entirely different side of the world, and began to like it."

"Aristocracy?"

"Not so much aristocracy itself as its influence. There was order. England at that time was very beautiful. After I left England, I had the notion of being always a student."

"A *vagans?*"

"Yes, but not exactly a wandering scholar—a knight errant—but not necessarily like Don Quixote (I noted the pronunciation: Kwiksot)—fighting imaginary enemies.

"Did you never rescue damsels in distress?"

"Never! Of course, at first it was hard. I hadn't much money. Later on I became rich, but it made no difference. I didn't change my way of life. Possessions are a burden. They anchor you to one place. Of course, when I had rooms at Harvard I decorated them. Do you know the Arundel prints?"*

"I've heard of them."

"They were engravings of the old masters, tinted. I had a Pinturruchio over my fireplace—very colorful, with beautiful costumes. In hotels where I lived, I couldn't do much—and I didn't want to. Here I have nothing to show. When I came to this place I was momentarily poor, but for all the sisters know I may still be poor—yet I'm rich. Money is important only in giving you a sense of a margin, and that you aren't a burden to anybody."

I had exhausted my questions of detail. I wished to close with one of principle, so I asked: "Do you think obscurity is an advantage to an intellectual?"

"A historian should not be obscure. He should be around where history is made." We discussed Hume as a philosopher who abandoned philosophy when the public refused to notice

*I believe the Medici prints were meant.

him. "Hume is important," said Santayana with a quizzical look, "—the analysis of consciousness." I pointed out that I didn't mean obscurity for historians alone, but for anyone following the spiritual life. We never could connect on this topic, so I judged Santayana was tired. I had a request to make. Could he let me have a copy of his last poems, together with PHILOSOPHERS AT COURT, etc.?

"The poems include what I call a *Testament*," said Santayana. "I want this book to be posthumous. Your book won't appear for some years, I suppose."

"Oh, no."

"Then you'll have plenty of time to read it. Besides, some of the poems in it are what Howard Sturgis called 'blushy'—you blush when you read them."

I assured him that, such being his wish, I was happy to abide by it, and deeply appreciated the opportunity he was giving me to read the unpublished portion of PERSONS AND PLACES.

I rose to go. "Tomorrow," I said, "I shall not call on you. I'm falling behind in my notes on PERSONS AND PLACES, and I want to finish them."

"When do you leave?"

"I'm leaving Tuesday, but I shall call on you Monday and Tuesday, if you like. Meanwhile, I hope you pass a very pleasant Easter."

"And thank you," he said, "for the roses. They haven't brought them back yet, have they?"

"Yes. There they are on the table." He approached them and I prepared to leave. As I was saying, "Goodbye," he turned and looked in my general direction. Suddenly the *bon vivant*, the witty *raconteur*, struck me as a helpless old man. It is true: he had looked in my direction, but obviously he saw nothing.

"I plan only to see you," I had written Santayana before I started my journey. "About the only things I haven't seen already in Rome are you and the Pope—and the Pope doesn't interest me: he is replaceable."

Occasionally I have had to remind my friends of this. So often they ask, "Didn't you see any night-life?"

Now, European night-life has a special meaning for Americans. It means teasing or fornicating in dives one wouldn't be seen dead in at home. Psychoanalysis via alcohol meant nothing to me. My nightly rounds, consequently, were tame. They consisted simply of short walks after dining at the *San Carlo*.

The *San Carlo* was one of three restaurants recommended by Santayana. I went no farther. The best food I have eaten I have found, first, in Vienna, next, in Mexico, and now here. I saw no reason to experiment in other directions. I always arrived around seven: early for Rome. Few guests were present. Often I found the *San Carlo* empty.

The waiters and manager and I soon became friends. The manager talked English and seemed ahead of his times. An a-typical bourgeois, this man seemed genuinely anxious about Italian unemployment: 2,000,000 out of work, he told me. The wealthy, he felt, are not enlightened. They refuse to follow principles of Christian charity. Surpluses exist in Italy but they are not distributed. Why, then, should anyone be surprised, he asked, at Communism?

Years before, his entire staff had emigrated to Mexico. Learning that I visited Mexico from time to time, he scribbled a greeting to the chef at the Prado and gave it to me to deliver.

One evening three well-groomed American girls entered and sat down near my table. Of course they ordered *pâté de foi gras*—not native to Italy, but imported from France. The waiters were in a swoon over all this glamour. Their excitement was carefully masked, however, except for one detail. One puny waiter concocted an Easter bunny out of a napkin held over his hand. To this he fed bits of parsley so that the girls could see it. His antics went on behind the back of the head-waiter who, meanwhile, was obsequiously serving the debutantes.

After dinner, I strolled about town for an hour. This was promenade time. Nothing more charming or fascinating than a Roman crowd out on promenade! It being the night before Easter, all churches were full. Worshippers entered by one door and filed out by another in endless processions.

On this night of the twenty-fourth, I returned to the hotel after my stroll. The nymphomaniac was there in the elevator, with one or two admirers pendant. "I've received so many flowers today," she gasped ecstatically. "You *must* come up and see my flowers!"

Around ten I left the hotel again, bound for St. Peter's, the vigil, and midnight mass.

The crowds thinned as I reached the Tiber embankment. No special illumination distinguished St. Peter's in the distance. A very solemn vigil, I thought to myself. Reaching the plaza in front of the basilica, I saw that it was dark. I walked past the obelisk which Caligula had brought from Heliopolis in the first century, then up to the great façade. Even the wrought-iron grills were locked. Not one burning candle showed from the inside. This, I began to think, is really odd. A few lone characters wandered about aimlessly. I stood perplexed, just as aimless as they.

A pretty girl of perhaps twenty-four approached me. She spoke in Italian. A few mumbled words of mine convinced her that I was no adept in that language. She changed to English— *English* English. "Isn't there a midnight mass," she inquired melodiously. "There doesn't seem to be a soul around."

I replied that I had expected to find a vigil going on, but had evidently been misinformed. After waiting a short while, we hit on the plan of asking the Swiss guards. None were visible, but to the left we could make out a lighted doorway. We entered and found a pair of guards on night-duty. The British girl—for such she was—asked about the vigil and the mass. The guards checked in the *Osservatore Romano*. New bishops were being ordained in St. John of the Lateran. A vigil and mass were being celebrated at *Santa Maria Maggiore*. Tomorrow, they said, Easter mass would be celebrated in St. Peter's at eleven, and the Pope would give the benediction at twelve.

Disappointed, the girl and I walked back toward the obelisk. She decided to take a taxi to *Santa Maria Maggiore*. "Here's where I join my party," she said. "Won't you come with us?" I thanked her, but decided not to intrude. I walked back slowly along the Tiber and home to the hotel.

As I entered the elevator, a boozy individual approached with the Zulu in tow, or was it the other way around? We were about to close the door when the night-clerk came running and said to the nymphomaniac: "You can't take him upstairs with you."

The Frenchwoman was the picture of righteous wrath. "Why not? I just want to show him my flowers. He comes up with me all the time. We'll be right down!"

"He can't go with you at this hour," the clerk insisted—making a rather fine point of morality, I fancied. As I have said, the *Albergo d'Inghilterra* is a decent hotel.

"He most certainly can," the Zulu replied. "I *won't* have rules made for my special benefit." This in a loud voice.

"Sh!" whispered her boozy companion, a rather seedy-looking blond. The Zulu was not to be shushed.

"Let me have your passport," said the clerk to the drunk, after a moment's indecision. The passport was handed over. The nymphomaniac rose toward her lair with her boozy prize.

As I left them on the third floor, he had managed again to say: "SH!"

MARCH 25, 1951: Easter

On Easter morning, as usual, I telephoned for breakfast to be served in my room. "*Caffé negro, per favore, e pan dolce.*"

"*Café complet?*" the clerk answered in French; then, in Italian, "*Si, signore.*"

At ten, I looked out the window. It was pouring! Not that I had actually come to Rome to see the replaceable Pope, but I had promised myself that I should hear mass at St. Peter's on Easter Sunday. I was especially anxious to hear the Vatican choir. Ten-thirty, and still no respite. After wavering, I put on my trench-coat and went out.

No sooner had I rounded the corner of the *Via dei Condotti* than the rain began to moderate. A few blocks farther, and the sun started breaking through the clouds. Along the Tiber the sun came out, bathing the dome of St. Peter's in glorious spring light. A miracle! I made my way through thickening crowds. As I neared the basilica, great bells began to ring.

Black, open carriages with red wheels were delivering pilgrims to the plaza. Swirling round the obelisk I saw every color of clerical habit: black, brown, gray, scarlet, purple—with every form of head-dress imaginable. One could take his pick of languages: German, French, Italian, Spanish—even Ethiopian. The basilica was jammed. In the apse, under Bernini's tumultuous sculptured clouds and the Throne of St. Peter, mass was proceeding. I stood next to the *baldacchino* of the high altar—not employed on this occasion. The choir was disappointing. Only the spectacle was magnificent.

After mass, a venerable Bishop—not the Pope—passed in procession. Shortly, on a balcony under the great dome, priests appeared exhibiting relics. Then the human tide bore me out to the front of the church. At one side in large window bays, priests of various orders were broadcasting the ceremony, speaking to their radio audience in many tongues. A man passed, bearing a large crucifix, to be blessed by the Pope. The papal band played hymns. Trumpets blared. On the balcony, over the papal banner, the Pope appeared. He spoke for about ten minutes, then gave the benediction. His listeners, not counting the radio audience, must have numbered hundreds of thousands, The plaza and all roofs within sight were full to overflowing.

The benediction over, I stood to one side watching the multitude disperse. The great bells of St. Peter's were almost turning over in their sockets. The Pope had prayed for peace. Would it come?

Once again after a grievous war I had snatched a glimpse of the Eternal City. I had seen the replaceable Pope, and Santayana—the irreplaceable.

MARCH 26, 1951

Vestiges of Easter flowers remained in the entrance-hall of the Convent of Blue Nuns. A great bouquet stood before *Maria Consolatrix Afflictorum*. Outside, however, in spite of brilliant sun and bursting greenery, a cold wind blew. I had just looked down on the Convent and *San Stefano* from the park across the *Via Claudia*—grounds of the Geographical Society. Either the entrance had been closed previously, or I had overlooked it. I regretted having no more film to take pictures from this coign of vantage. It was the best possible one for vistas of the Convent.

At the left window, as usual, sat Santayana. A magazine lay in his hand.

"I found out," I announced, "why I arrived so early Saturday and interrupted your meal."

"Why was that?"

"My watch was fast."

"No matter."

"Here, sir," I continued, "are all the chapters but one of PERSONS AND PLACES." I thanked him for the great privilege it had been to read them, and promised to bring the missing chapter tomorrow. This alone, I said, had rewarded me for the trip. I stated that the third part was the best of the three, and would arouse much comment.

"I shouldn't have thought so," Santayana said.

Thereupon I mentioned several parts I thought would awake public interest, including the *Travels*.

"You will end up in Baedeker," I quipped.

"I wasn't conscious of being original," Santayana remarked. "Maybe I came out of Baedeker in the first place!"

Then I told how fearful I had been, especially at corners where buses turned, because they might knock me down and destroy the precious copy.

"There are other copies," he said. "Cory has one, and then the manuscript is somewhere—perhaps in the next room. I have many French books there, behind the first row."

"Censored!" I cried.

"You'd never know I had them, and they cleaned house the other day, and everything is very orderly."

In an access of trite phrases, I exclaimed, "And you can't find a thing!"

"But if you'd been killed," he went on, "you really would not have had to worry!"

I agreed.

"Then one can always advertise. Ha! I see my name is on the envelope, so it would have been returned if the person who found it wanted to be kind!"

"Well," I concluded, "if it had been my manuscript, I should have been uneasy till I got it back."

Then I related the episode of the midnight vigil before St. Peter's.

"I'm sorry I misdirected you," said Santayana.

"Not at all! Didn't I meet that little girl? And Sunday, at eleven, I heard Mass at St. Peter's. Some Bishop celebrated that, but at twelve, the Pope spoke from a balcony."

"Did he speak? He usually just gives the Benediction."

I told how he had spoken for at least ten minutes, in Italian, which I understood fairly well. Then he had given the Benediction in Latin.

"It probably wasn't a good oration," observed Santayana.

"On the contrary," I said. "He's quite eloquent."

"Oh, that! They're trained in it."

"His gestures were dramatic"—here I demonstrated—"and he spoke without notes."

"They memorize it," Santayana said, "and then he always says the same thing."

I agreed that the substance seemed merely Peace and Welcome to pilgrims. Santayana remarked that the loud-speakers usually distorted his voice. I replied that the amplification had been excellent. The crowd had been enormous. One thing I *had* objected to. Some priests had tried to stimulate cheers for *il pappa* artificially.

"That's the political side," Santayana sighed. "They want to make the Catholics feel at home—that they're not hunted for being different."

He held up the magazine he had in his lap. It was THE HUMANIST.

"I've been reading this. I don't know why they send it to me. There's an article in it defending John Dewey. I don't know what Dewey means: he's always talking about 'relations' and 'conditions.' Why doesn't he give an example? Maybe he isn't clear in his own mind, and he's handicapped. He always has to start with America. Now, if he would give some examples from American business enterprise—but perhaps he doesn't know any. Babbitt used to give good historical examples . . ."

"Didn't you talk about him somewhere?"

"I wrote a whole book about him—THE GENTEEL TRADITION AT BAY."

"The tradition—but no longer at bay?" I asked. "Is this the same bunch?"

"No, this is a new crowd. They're political. Babbitt was at least a scholar." Santayana alluded to some classic which Babbitt had translated. "Corliss Lamont has an article in it (THE HUMANIST). It's not good."

Santayana began to narrate an anecdote, then checked himself. "Was I telling you about it? . . ."

"No."

"Oh, it was Coolidge—yesterday."

"Then the young man came!"

"Yes, and he brought three others with him. Cory was here too, so we had to move books off chairs for people to sit down."

"That was one reason," I said, "why I stayed away yesterday. I was sure you would have numerous visitors."

Santayana went on to mention how Coolidge was teaching at Lyons, and had been to Arras. Also, that two of the boys had sat there, almost mute, necessarily—like extras on a stage. When Cory brought his wife, all Santayana heard from her, he said, was "tweet, tweet, tweet." We agreed that we had succeeded in communicating fairly well, at close range. Only once, I said, had he heard me say "barbarous" and answered, "I should go to the barber." (See above, page 35.)

"I couldn't have said that," he objected, "because I never go. I cut my own now. I never did like to go to the barber. Once in a while it was pleasant, but not often. I did like Turkish baths . . . I even cut my own toe-nails. For an old man, toe-nails are a problem. You can't bend over. Maria (*the maid*) said the Sisters would do it for me, but I still do it. Cory brought me a special pair of scissors for the purpose . . ."

Our conversation was limping—on toe-nails—but only later did I learn why.

I hauled out my questionnaire. First I checked on the order of the chapters in Part III of PERSONS AND PLACES. Then I reverted to a question I had written him, but had received no answer for. He was with Loeser once in a museum, he had written in PERSONS AND PLACES. There he had remarked, in front of one painting, "I'd like to paint like that!"

"What," I inquired, "was the painting?" After all, Santayana's preferences in art were significant, at least in the light of the BOHEMIAN PROTEST, the series of which his biography would be the last.

"I don't remember the painter," Santayana replied. "It was a classical subject, but by a modern painter. Loeser said he would help me if I wanted to paint, but I couldn't give up my work at Harvard for that. Besides, although he didn't say how much, he would have helped me generously—but he might have got tired. Then, as my father said, I was good in design but had no touch. I liked color—not spotty—: big washes. I should have liked to paint the SYMPOSIUM—but of course, that was at night."

"What difference would that make?"

"Oh, I suppose Rembrandt could do it—but I'm not Rembrandt." He added that he did not care for portraits as expressions of art.

I inquired if he sketched architecture much. When he was a boy, he said, he planned whole churches, with ground-plan, front elevation and perspective. Furthermore, he said, people who say landscape must have figures forget that figures need landscape, or at least background—a natural setting.

Santayana also used to plan houses—different versions of the kind he would have liked to live in. The ground floor would have a little entrance-hall, a morning-room, dining-room and servants' quarters. A twin stairway that turned and came together would form an *entresol*. His bed-room and a guest bed-room would open from this, while the stairway proceeded up to a spacious living-room between—a room serving also as the library. A mansard above would hold bed-rooms for the servants.

"And your study?" I asked.

"For reading," he said, "I should use the living-room—for writing the bed-room. I should have a pretty bed-room."

He mentioned Berenson's Empire bed-room in Florence. It was beautiful—with canopied bed like a sofa, apparently seldom slept in. Berenson, he added, had sent him the book on Tibet, and had written the preface.

"It's a small thing," Santayana commented. "He knows nothing about Tibet." I had noticed Berenson's HISTORY AND AESTHETICS on the book-shelf. Santayana hadn't got into the book. A recent autobiographical work by Berenson, he said, was quite bad.

I brought up Edmund Wilson's article about Santayana. It had suggested that he had written THE IDEA OF CHRIST in order simply to have something to do when he was without books during the war.

"Oh, no," he replied. "I had many books—those you see here. My others were in boxes here in Rome, but I hadn't had them sent over. One didn't know how long the war would last."

"Did you have the idea for the book long before?"

"No. I never thought of writing a book on Christ."

I mentioned a passage in PERSONS AND PLACES where he and Warwick Potter had been discussing the humanity and divinity of Christ. This had taken place in the Nineteenth Century. Santayana was interested, but insisted that the idea of the book had come to him recently.*

"I read the Bible through," he said. "I didn't like it so much. The Sisters gave me their English version of the Vulgate. It doesn't read so well as the King James Version—which was translated from the originals."

Referring again to his talks with Potter, I asked, "Isn't the theme simply incarnation?"

"Yes," he replied. "How could Christ be divine? It could only be ideally. Man can only become like God in idea—just as God can only become man by *thinking* of man: otherwise there would be no distinction of parts."

"Like extension in Descartes?"

"Yes. The two natures alternated in Christ. One was usually in abeyance, but it was there. Sometimes it broke through, as in the scene where they let the man down to be healed. 'Thy sins are forgiven thee,' Christ said—not thinking. Immediately there was an outcry: 'Blasphemy!' "

"He was talking like God."

"So he asked, 'Is it easier to say, "Thy sins are forgiven thee" or "Take up thy bed and walk"?' You see, he forgot, and betrayed his divinity. Then, at the marriage of Cana . . .'"

"Oh, yes!—the regal gesture," I cried, "turning water into the *best* wine . . .'"

"There's some by-play in that scene," said Santayana, "where Mary is asking him to do it. 'Oh, why do you bother me?' he asks. 'It's none of our affair.' The translation is perhaps questionable. In the original it reads: 'What is this to me, to you?' In another scene, after his death, which I'm told not everyone has
*But cp. Santayana's letter of Jan. 10, 1952, p. 160f.

noticed, he appears to the Apostles. At first he stands in a darkened doorway, watching them fish. They're catching nothing. 'Have you meat?' he asks, and they answer, 'No.' 'Try the other side of the boat,' he suggests. They do, and take out so many hundred fish. Then John says, 'It's the Lord!' Meanwhile Christ has prepared food and a fire on shore, and the Apostles dress. Peter swims out. He's naked. Then he puts on his cloak—but he can't eat. There is the business about founding the Church on him and feeding the flock—the way it's inscribed in the dome of St. Peter's."

"In the third part of PERSONS AND PLACES," I said, "you mention that Paris is a good place to watch the dissolution of Christendom: still, the other day, when I asked about Christianity's future, you said it would last for this aeon, at any rate. Would you care to say something about that?"

"I meant that France is no longer Catholic. You don't feel the presence of religion there. It's not part of the people's daily life. I don't see how Duron can work in the Ministry of Instruction. And Coolidge tells me that education is very anticlerical. I never had a French friend. Oh, of course, there was Mme. Fontenay, wife of the ambassador . . ."

Here followed a discussion of pseudo-religion among women. It involved, among others, the Strongs and Rockefellers and the Mme. Blanc-Blanc of PERSONS AND PLACES, who was really a Mme. Finternat. Also of her son's marital intentions, there related, and of his training Polish troops.

"Evidently," laughed Santayana, "he didn't do so well. He may even have been killed."

The name, Rockefeller, led easily to my next question. Santayana had spoken of Sassoon, in England, as one of many melancholy Jews who masqueraded as magnates, like the Rockefellers and Astors!

"That was one part which I thought might be indiscreet," he admitted. "Perhaps I shouldn't have put it in." (This passage was deleted from the first edition of MY HOST THE WORLD.)

"Rockefeller and Astor weren't Jews, were they?"

"No. Rockefeller was a Baptist. That was the connection between him and Strong."

Santayana went on to say that Strong, who had nothing in common with the Fontenays, had invited them to stay a week at Fiesole. They came—nobody knew why, unless it was economy. A week as someone's guest, Santayana remarked, would mean a great saving to them. Strong had made a list of subjects for conversation on a card.

"Did you enjoy talking with them?" Santayana had asked him.

"Oh, very much," Strong had replied.

Here I wondered if Santayana were poking sly fun at my card of questions. I glanced at it hastily and put it away. Only one question remained: about Gandhi. The talk had drifted to Buddhism—a sect in it being like the early Christian church.

"That seems to be the fate of them," I observed. "The institution grows up and smothers the original spirit. See what happened to Confucius in China!"

I told about a recent book which purported to show that the real Confucius had been buried in tradition and niceties of imperial protocol.

"I don't care for Confucius," said Santayana. "He's commonplace. Oh, he modelled Chinese society on the family, and taught respect for age and of the younger brother for the elder brother . . . In such a society, where people know their place, there is a chance for individual happiness. But the Chinese philosopher I like is . . ."

"Lao-Tse?"

"Yes. He was a real philosopher—that is, a hermit. He thought for himself. He wasn't part of a school."

"What do you think of Gandhi?" This question was important to me, because Gandhi, together with Lenin, were two world figures—according to Howgate—whom Santayana had never mentioned. A look of distaste crossed Santayana's face.

"I've never kept in touch with politics," he began. "Gandhi

seems to have used religion—the old religious feeling of India, brought it up to date—and used it for political purposes."

I was not surprised at this. Santayana was a Tory. Churchill had called Gandhi an East Indian fakir, and refused to meet him. Anything attacking England—Tory England—would naturally be anathema.

However, I mentioned Gandhi's idea of "war without violence." Santayana seemed interested but unconvinced. I had intended bringing up Lenin, but after this, refrained. (Lenin *is* alluded to in DOMINATIONS AND POWERS.)

We turned then to discussing various editions of Santayana's books. Glancing at the title-page of one volume, Santayana said, "I wanted to change this George to Jorge later on, but nobody (in America) would know how to pronounce it—and I *was* named after a George—my mother's *first* husband." (We laughed.) "I don't know how she managed that, except that my father had no retrospective jealousy. He once said to me about George Sturgis, 'He was a simpleton.' And there was something of that in the family. My half-sister, Josefina, wasn't right. She was like a child."

"And Susana?"

"She was a mistake. Mother didn't care for her."

"Religion?"

"No. My mother was mourning Pepe, the boy who died. Susana wasn't blonde, and she didn't have blue eyes—like Pepe. And Pepe was unselfish. He was already dying, so he didn't care. He gave his toys to the baby. Naturally Susana took them. Susana always wanted to be somebody, if only in Avila— but what's that?"

I complimented him on the large print in his books. "I had nothing to do with it," he answered. "I had good publishers."

I then deplored Duron's fine print, but Santayana said it was a huge book and expensive. "I wrote him," he stated, "congratulating him on getting it published at all. It will be the standard work on me, if anyone wants to read it—which I suppose won't be many." Santayana himself had only read the end—*"Difficulties"*—and said Duron was very accurate and had stuck close to the text.

Santayana then mentioned that he had been sick—vomited, mainly bile— the previous night. The cakes, with citrous fruit pieces, which he had eaten at tea the day before, had upset him. The maid, trying to be helpful, had brought him brandy around ten at night to settle his stomach. It had made him worse. So she had brought him something else. He had thrown up and felt relieved. I offered to go, so that he could rest.

"Oh, I recover very quickly," he said. He didn't seem to want me to leave, so I lingered a few minutes.

"Twice," I said, "since I've been here you seemed low."

"Yes," he assented. "It's mainly the weather. Now it's beautiful, and I feel better. You see, I keep the window open."

Having reached the weather as a topic for further conversation, I realized it would be a kindness for me to retire. For my convenience, Santayana arranged for me to call on him tomorrow during the forenoon—in order that I shouldn't have to hurry to catch my plane.

MARCH 27, 1951

"I was asleep," said Santayana as he opened the door. "I was sick, you know, night before last."

"Did you spend a bad night again?" I asked.

"No. I rested well, until about five. I was dozing again when you knocked."

"When do you have breakfast?"

"At seven-thirty—but I like to be washed before that."

"I'm afraid that company you had Sunday upset you."

"No doubt, no doubt."

"I have brought back the final chapter," I said, "and want to thank you again."

"Very well. Last night I was reading FAREWELL TO ENGLAND, and I'm dissatisfied with it. It's not well organized. I repeat things: how Russell changed toward me, and all that."

"The part about Santayana and Sargeaunt?" (Russell, in his later years, had mixed up the names.)

"Yes. I think I can compress it and turn it around. I think I can do it, and I'll have it retyped. The chapter about Howard Sturgis seemed all right."

This had also been my opinion. Lest I should forget, I retrieved my manuscripts. He had forgotten they were on his desk. He regretted he hadn't read them all, and I regretted the faint type. Especially to be deplored, I felt, was his inability to read the cosmological chapter from POE. That chapter was jinxed! Some years before, I had sent a copy to Whitehead—only to learn that the sage had just died. Now another, capable of judging the chapter's merits, was incapacitated. *Kismet!*

"I'm going to send you THE MEETING OF EAST AND WEST," I said. "I hope the print isn't too fine."

"I have trouble with newspapers," said Santayana—he was reading IL TEMPO before I came—"but if the book is interesting, I'll read it."

"It has a wonderful chapter on Mexico," I told him, "the best I've ever seen."

"*Your* book," he stated, "should be there when you get home."

"What book is that?"

"My latest. I was hoping a reviewer's copy would arrive. I was supposed to receive three, but I told them to send you one when the author's presentation copy comes out. How long does it take from New York—three days?"

"Not more."

"Well, then, you see: it will reach you before mine gets here—because that takes at least a week."

I thanked him for his great kindness. He said he hoped the book was in the bright red cover, not the usual brownish one. Also, that the dust-cover would be attractive. One which Robert Lowell had possessed—REALMS OF BEING—had carried a caption under a picture: "George Santayana writing this book."

"I wasn't writing," he laughed. "Somebody who visited me

asked to take a picture of me writing, so I sat at the table, pretending."

One reviewer, I remembered, had said on a jacket of THE LAST PURITAN: "This is for a reader who wishes to think while he reads."

"But that is a compliment!" he exclaimed.

I was reminded in turn of the curious passage toward the end of THE LAST PURITAN where Santayana introduces a fourth dimension, *Eternity*. I commented on how unusual it was and how much I had enjoyed it. Also the symbolism of Oliver watching Jim Darnley dive into the ocean—symbolism only explained toward the end.

"Where Oliver is wondering whether you can sense in advance what is to happen?"

"Yes."

"That is the story seen as truth."

"A different perspective? I felt as if we had suddenly turned the opera-glasses around."

"Yes. The present includes the past and the future, and in a sense it is all three—the relativity of time. For the past, the present is the future, and so on. In a sense the present is everywhere. Bergson—I don't like him for his anti-intellectuality and his appeal to emotion and feeling—but Bergson says something in MATIÈRE ET MÉMOIRE: 'In memory the past exists always as it was.' That is, it *would* if we had perfect memories. The part I like about Bergson here is the mystical side. The idea is clear enough, and one could say: 'Well, what about it?' and never feel a thing."

This called to my mind Henry James' BERKELEY SQUARE. There time is likened to a winding river. If one could rise high enough—that is, to the point of view of eternity—all time would seem as one.

"The same idea," Santayana agreed.

Then I asked him about Whitehead's "objective immortality"—for I knew that together, Santayana and I were immortalizing this moment. I explained that, objectively, everything makes a *difference,* and so goes on forever.

Santayana agreed at first—then had an after-thought. "The trouble is that the difference finally gets drowned in all kinds of irrelevant relations."

"Gradually," I acknowledged, "it fades." Our case for immortality on the material plane was growing weaker and weaker. I changed the subject.

"Have you any recommendations," I asked, "for correcting common misrepresentations about you?"

"No," he said. "I haven't been badly misrepresented. Oh, I got one or two complaining letters, but in general nothing."

"I was thinking about the notices LIFE and TIME have written about you."

"You can't expect anything from newspapers," he exclaimed. "Reporters never get what I say right."

"I recall the review in TIME about your IDEA OF CHRIST. They were very smug. What was Luce: a missionary?" (Henry Luce: publisher of LIFE and TIME.)

"I don't know."

"In any case, they said that after a lifetime of scepticism you had returned to the faith you abandoned."

"That's not true! I haven't changed. Of course, I have always favored Catholicism—but the Catholics object to me because to me the dogma is not literal truth, but simply valid poetry."

Here Santayana digressed into his customary views on the symbolic nature of human faculties.

"I see us," he said, "as insects with limited senses and faculties. All round lies the greater reality, which we can never grasp fully—but religion can be a symbol of this."

He repeated the Jacob's Ladder story. "If one takes the parables, by themselves, in the New Testament, it appears that Christ was making the same distinction between the Lord, *i.e.* the one who generated you, and God, whom you worship if he takes care of you. I don't like the word, creation. To create, you must have an idea in advance and simply carry it out.

Generation is a better word—like the little girl who, when someone said, 'God made you,' answered, 'No, I grew.' "

Santayana cited the proverb: "To him who hath shall be given," as an example of God as *nature*—not necessarily just to, or interested in, human justice. The parable about payment of a penny for one or six hours' work, the parable of the prodigal son, and of the eleventh hour guest represented *grace*—or God looking after his worshippers like a generous monarch.

"If I were writing a LIFE OF CHRIST, which I should never do," said Santayana, "I should use the parables as an example of the distinction I make between Nature and Essence. Jesus was making them, although his listeners didn't know it. Of course," he added, "there's fair evidence that Christ is a legend." He cited two works by Couchoud.

"That," he said, "does not affect the spiritual significance of the Gospels. I like the oldest and newest Gospels best: that is, Mark and John. In Mark the details are about a man. In John he is a god and a church has been established—but the two Gospels are inwardly consistent."

I mentioned the legendary character of all religion. Buddhism, he thought, was less human in its details about the Buddha than Christianity about Christ. He had not heard the story of *La Virgen de Guadalupe*, as told by Northrop. I explained how, on the very spot where Juan Diego was supposed to have seen his vision, the Indians had worshipped a virgin goddess before Cortez. Santayana countered with mention of *Maria sopra Minerva* here in Rome, and *La Virgen del Pilar* in Saragossa.

"St. James was on his way to Compostella," he said, "when the Virgin appeared to him. Of course there is doubt that St. James was ever in Spain or got out of Jerusalem—but the legend is that he went. He *had* to go, because he was going to die there!"

"That's a pretty good reason," I remarked.

"A good reason to be *taken*!" Santayana snorted, "but he should have said '*Don't* take me to Spain!' "

The diminutive virgin *del pilar*, he said, was dressed in a long, round skirt so as to be seen from a distance. The figure was no bigger than a doll. The pillar is kissed to this day by Spaniards, whose patron saint is, of course, St. James.

"Sargent painted the virgin that way," I reminded him, "for the Boston library."

"He would! Sargent would always do the thing archaeologically. It isn't wrong, you know, when they paint the apostles in Greek robes. That was the Hellenistic period, and Jerusalem was Greek. Of course, it's just as likely that they dressed as the Arabs do now, with a turban on their heads."

As a precaution against future disaster, I requested Cory's address, which Santayana wrote down for me. I had never made the acquaintance of Cory, as I planned. Santayana seemed to have some purpose in keeping us apart, and I did not press the matter. It well may be that he didn't want Cory to find out that I had read *his* copy of part three of PERSONS AND PLACES! Cory's mailing address was in London—a banking firm of Santayana's as well. I said that it might happen that he, Santayana, would be indisposed, and unable to write. Cory could send me news about him.

"You can make him write," Santayana grinned, "by asking about me. Of course, I'll write you if I'm able."

"I want you to know," I said, "that my experience here runs contrary to what often happens. I have watched your work for twenty years—ever since Harvard."

"You know a great deal."

"I intend to know a lot more so as to do you justice. But it often happens that when one makes the personal acquaintance of such a person—one whom he has admired at a distance— disillusion takes place."

"I wasn't always," said Santayana wistfully, glancing at his person, "as I am now."

"I know that and see that. It has been no disillusionment for me. And I shall be happy to report back in the States that certain stories of your feebleness aren't true. Obviously, if you can't hear well, you can't follow a conversation from across the room, of a reporter who sits politely at arm's length. Also, if you can't see well, you aren't able to read lips."

"No, I can't do that."

"So, it isn't hard to understand how you might lose the thread."

"Oh, but I do lose the thread—very often, and even when I'm alone. Sometimes before I'm across the room I forget what I started for."

"That happens to anybody."

"I wasn't always like that. Now, when I'm shaving, I must do everything in the same order. Otherwise I don't know if I did it. The same with brushing my teeth. I sometimes look to see if the toothbrush is wet."

"When you make things unconscious like that, and automatic, you free yourself for other things."

"I suppose so. And the mind remains young regardless of what happens to the body."

"You are a young man," I asserted. "When I was asked about you at home I showed your first letter. The handwriting is steady and the thought is coherent. And I'm confident you are going to write that book on Alexander."

I saw from my watch that I must go. We lingered for a moment on the subject of forgetfulness. I told a story about my father and a colleague of his, who absent-mindedly wore two vests to work. In telling the story I almost alluded to my father by his right name—not Lind; but caught the slip in time—not that it would have done great damage at this time, for Santayana is really not prejudiced against Germans, I had found —only merciless and fair toward their short-comings.

Hearing my father mentioned, Santayana said, "You have told me nothing about yourself or your family. I have spent the whole time egotistically talking about myself."

"There's not much to tell," I said, and gave him a brief synopsis of my career. My work with the Veterans' Administration, I said, was like the trade he had recommended for philosophers: taking umbrellas in a museum. He said he hoped

I might tell him more some time, and I promised to write other details, if he wished.

"Then, one of these days," he said, "you will be getting married."

"I'm forty-one," I retorted, "and a confirmed bachelor."

This surprised him. He had thought I was in my thirties. "Well," he said, "if you're *that* old . . ." and proceeded to narrate an anecdote concerning a dinner party, where he had remarked that at forty-nine one doesn't marry with impunity. "But that's when *I* married!" exclaimed the lady next to him.

"Then perhaps," he said to me, "you will be back."

"In one or two years," I said, "if possible. I have every motive to return."

With a few more formalities we parted. I left him seated, as usual, with his blanket around his knees, in the chair by the left window.

On the way back to the hotel I retraced meditatively the exact path I had taken to the Convent of Blue Nuns, two short weeks ago. Rome was beautiful, and—I thought—would always be beautiful, with its stalwart pines, its venerable ruins, and the young life springing up between. Rome, with Santayana as part of my memory of it, would remain for me classically gay forever: not immune to vicissitudes of Fate, surely, but—like Olympus—essentially a place of

> *Heavenly laughter, shaking from its wings*
> *Atoms of light, and tears for mortal things.*

III. CORRESPONDENCE, July 5, 1951—July 18, 1952

S TOPPING in New York on the way home, I called Stechert-Hafner, the book importers, and asked them to send Santayana a copy of Northrop's THE MEETING OF EAST AND WEST. Once settled again in San Antonio, I wrote Stechert, confirming the order. Shortly I received a bill for *two* copies of Northrop, plus a volume by Robinson Jeffers which I had also ordered for Santayana. I wrote my friend that he was about to receive the books, including duplicates—so as not to confuse him. I also acknowledged receipt of a presentation copy of DOMINATIONS AND POWER, which he had had Scribners send to me.

My first concern was to transcribe our dialogues, index them, and write the "interludes"—accounts of the days in Rome when I was not interviewing Santayana.

Meanwhile, reviews of DOMINATIONS AND POWERS were appearing. Few hit the bull's eye. The majority seemed to me sophomoric. I wrote Santayana in this vein: "From reading numerous half-baked reviews of your book, I gather that few people, even now, understand you. I believe I know the reason: you write too well, and say what you mean. That's very confusing, you know. We're not used to it." I was thinking in particular of a friend of mine, a writer of no mean ability, who had waded through DOMINATIONS AND POWERS. "I tried to understand it," she jested. "It was a good fight, but I lost." To me, the message of Santayana seemed clear and forthright. I proceeded to write a review of it myself. The English-speaking papers in San Antonio had no space for so lengthy an article, but LA PRENSA, the Spanish daily, took the review in translation. It appeared on two successive days, June 26th and 27th, 1951. I sent the review to Santayana, and received shortly the following reply—a valuable commentary, it seems to me, on his book. I was pleased to note that he had dropped the *Mr.* from my name.

Via Santo Stefano Rotondo, 6,
Rome, 5th of July, 1951

Dear Lind

Your article—is it written by you in Spanish or translated by someone else?—especially the latter part of it, puts the "solution" of the present political problem that I *suggest*, but do not expect to have history exemplify. It is too simple and final, as the real solutions in history (or evasions and abandonments of a solution) never are. It would give a fairer notion of my philosophy to mention that I approach the question psychologically, by studying what the various real interests are in human life: and from that point of view divide the just adaptation of our wills to physical powers from the *impossible* adaptation of them to a single *ideal* good or purpose which does not exist at all, either above the universe or at the root of all our natures *identically*. It is therefore my general philosophy that leads me to that "dichotomy," not my political hopes, which I think can only be specific and of short range.

That is the point I should like to have made in explanation of my daring to propose *a solution* of our difficulties at all.

There is an objection that I expect will often be raised to this dichotomy. I say that the economic and legal order can be justly imposed by science and an international disinterested police, while moral, social, and religious life should be free for every individual or group to develop separately, according to its taste and genius. But, as I myself have pointed out somewhere, we are *more* gregarious mentally than materially. A man may prefer to walk alone over the mountains, but he hates to stand alone in his principles or opinions. I may seem, in my book, to have overlooked this desire to be unanimous ideally. If you take notice of my proposal, however, you will find that I speak of "moral societies," "moral units" in the midst of a single economic and police system and control. Religious and liberal arts will all be *social*, both in space and time; but they will be many and not easily sympathetic to one another. The continuity of any ideal science or art binds the generations of religious and artistic minds of each sort together, as may their flocking together with enthusiasm in each age—I value "club spirit" as much as "team work" but I want *many* clubs, many arts and kinds of music. G.S.

Note: I hadn't understood that it was *you* that sent me Jeffers' and Northrup's books. The latter has not been duplicated; but by chance I have got into touch with him personally, through his son! And Jeffers himself has sent me a copy of his "Double Axe," which I have read. Many thanks.

On July 31st, 1951, I wrote Santayana again, posing certain questions. The two which he had found time to answer are quoted below:

"A certain perspective is beginning to establish itself in my mind," I wrote him, "with respect to REALMS OF BEING. Your analogy between realms of being and the Persons of the Trinity is no accident, I feel sure. Catholicism undergoes strange metamorphoses. It would not surprise me," I joked, "could I return to earth three hundred years from now, to learn that San Jorge de Santillana had lately been canonised: long beyond the pale, but now recognized as the Aquinas who reinterpreted the doctrine of the Trinity in the light of the ancient human orthodoxy he discovered in the twentieth century. Actually, I have a question for you. Do you think your doctrine could pass without violence into the Catholic tradition? And a corollary: Do you think Catholicism has a future if it does not embody at least the most important of your insights?"

During our conversations, Santayana had mentioned a certain Roberts, with whom he travelled at one time in Germany. There is a Roberts also mentioned in PERSONS AND PLACES. I wondered if he was the same individual. Santayana's reply follows:

Via Santo Stefano Rotondo, 6,
Rome, 3 October, 1951

Dear Lind

Your letter of July 31st was answered at once, but I got it back after a longish interval, marked in red pencil "A better address" ("wanted," understood). I compared the address I had written down with that in your letter and could (with my bad astigmatism) discover no difference. Yesterday, however, when I showed Cory the envelope and your given address, he saw at once that I had written 525 University Avenue instead of 325. I am sorry, as there were points in my reply to you that I ought not to have left apparently unanswered.

The Roberts mentioned in "Persons and Places" was a school friend of Russell's, whom I saw only once in a room with other people, when he had become a teacher of mathematics in some school, but had been mentioned in Lady Scott's first law suit against Russell—with scandalous insinuations. *My* friend Roberts was much younger, one of my pupils about 1910, Thornton Roberts of New York, who had been at St. Paul's School, and afterwards spent a year or two at Christ Church, Oxford, rowing for the college. He was a critical self-reliant man and not quite normal. His last letter to me was quite insane, and I never was able to trace him afterwards, and feared he might be in an asylum. In these last years, however, I have had a correspondence with a lady who said she was a niece of his, and asked for my sentiments and knowledge about him. He had been living in an obscure hotel on the West Side of the Park, quite alone and friendless, and reported to take opium. A sad end, but one not impossible to explain in view of his constitutional solipsism. But he had very fine perceptions and insights about other people.

I hope you will not go in your book into the possibility of my replacing Aristotle as the accepted Pagan philosopher for Catholics. The Church is founded on Judaism; it accepts a naturalism with miraculous powers secretly controlling it, and controlling each soul. My naturalism does not admit a moral or humanistic control over the cosmos; and it puts spirit at the top, an accidental ultimate self-awakening of organic formations, themselves perfectly automatic. Spirit comes and goes in the world like dew in the morning. That is not compatible with the supernatural realism and monarchial theism of the Church.

There is another friend of mine, Prof. Michele Petrone, who thinks that my views might, if understood, start a sort of new spiritual discipline: but I think they offer too sporadic and unfruitful a consummation to satisfy mankind. Nietsche said: "The great question is whether mankind can endure the truth."

Yours sincerely,

G. Santayana

A rather abrupt turn in my personal affairs intervened between the foregoing letter and the next. The extracts which follow are, I think, self-explanatory. On October 29, 1951, I wrote Santayana:

"Please note the new address.

"My father, who has just retired, is with me now. We have been in the process of disposing of his property up in St. Louis and buying a house here: each phase took approximately two months. Had it not been for the confusion ensuing I should have written you before now . . .

"Here . . . is a biographical query. Although, in general, you disclaim being any one of your characters in THE LAST PURITAN, am I right or wrong in guessing that Oliver's decision to stay in America with his mother, rather than voyage with his father, resembles your own decision as a youth? I feel here a decision between the heart and the head—and the head won."

In one of the most important letters for any future biographer, Santayana replied:

Via Santo Stefano Rotondo, 6
Rome. 29 November, 1951

Dear Lind

I have been, and am, rather ill, and I don't remember whether I have answered your letter of October 29th with its interesting personal news and questions. But I feel like straightening out a little, even if I have already written something about it, the relation of myself and my family feelings to "The Last Puritan." That book contains all my experience of human life and character. But the moral "essences" are manifested in entirely different circumstances and careers than those in which I "intuited" them. For instance, Oliver's choice between his father and mother is a free choice. Both careers were open, and he chose the less alluring one because he was a Puritan. I had no real choice. Staying with my father in Spain was *impossible*, and he never proposed (it) to me, although ideally, if it had been possible, both he and I would have preferred it. For Oliver it was a sacrifice, not for his mother's sake, as you see later, in the scenes in the steamer returning to America after his father's death. He had and he showed no sympathy with his mother but bitterly enjoyed defeating her plans.

The relation between Peter and his wife was *emotionally* based on that between my father and mother, but *historically* the two cases are contraries. He had the money in the novel; she had it in real life, what little there was of it. But my father if he had been very rich and yet independent of the world (which would not have been possible in Spain where there were a few rich landholders with complicated family and political duties, like the Duke of Alba, whose agent for the Province of Aosta was my brother-in-law, but no free capitalists)—if my father had been rich he would have lived much as Peter did, and would have behaved towards me as Peter did to Oliver. But I was more like my father (and like Peter) than Oliver was like his: for he really was more like his mother, only genuine and not sham in his virtue. And my mother was not like his. She was silent and indifferent in minor matters, and stoical. But the absence of affection all round was the same in both mothers and in both husbands and in both sons. You will do right if you see the shadow of myself and my family in the book, but must not assimilate the circumstances. It was perhaps exactly a reversal, in a dream, of the circumstances of my life, while preserving the characters, that produced the novel.

Mr. Wheelock, of Scribners, has induced Cory and me to undertake making a one-volume work out of the five vols. of "The Life of Reason," revised and abridged. I have now read half the book and marked 1/3 of Vol. I, and 1/6 of Vol II to be removed; and Vol III is even less deserving of mutilation. We both find the thing better written than we had supposed; but we must nerve ourselves up to condense whole pages and chapters, as well as all the overworked words of that day: experience, practice, progress, consciousness, etc. "Creative" luckily was not yet the fashion.

Congratulations on your new family life.

G. Santayana

"In view of your illness,'" I replied to the above letter on December 5, 1951, "I was touched to hear from you at all. I'm sure were I in a similar case, that I should neglect everybody. Moreover, I was appalled at the magnitude of the task you have set for yourself in revising The Life of Reason . . . And now, as last year, let me be among the first to congratulate you on your coming birthday. I hope you pass it happily and *quietly*, so that you aren't upset as you were with all those visitors last Easter . . . Recently I obtained micro-films of your early poems, the ones you entrusted to Buffalo University. I also wrote the Library of Congress for your sonnet: At Arles. They replied that I must obtain your written permission, so I am enclosing a letter (to save you trouble) which, if you wish, you may send to the man in charge, releasing your sonnet from bondage."

Before receiving a reply to the foregoing, the Library of Congress sent me the desired photostats, and I wrote Santayana, thanking him for his courtesy. I also mentioned a sonnet sequence I was writing—a tribute to Catholicism by a heretic—entitled VIA CRUCIS. I had thought of dedicating it to him, embodying in the dedication a hint to the reader that the author was not one of the fold:

TO SANTAYANA

Ah, who can tell
how, from your hermit's cell
the Way of the Cross
appears:
if it weave a spell,
vanquish the years
with love, or—like Icarus —
start tears?

Santayana replied promptly, but made a mistake in my address, with the result that his letter was returned. Eventually I received two letters, a day apart, and delivered backward, chronologically speaking. The one, dated January 10, I received a day after the other, dated February 23. I reproduce them here in their proper order. The first is concerned with Santayana's sonnet, the second with my sequence which, on first reading, did not please him.

> Via S. Stefano Rotondo, 6,
> Rome, Jan. 10, 1952

Dear Lind:

The enclosed letter has just arrived, and makes me wonder at the complexity of life now in the U.S. It was much simpler in my early days. It occurred to me at once when you first wrote, including a typed letter for me to sign, to the Photographic Department in the Library of Congress, how easily I could have sent you a copy of that sonnet—only 14 lines!— which I have a copy of, and besides know by heart. It is not a good sonnet considered as a work of classic poetic art, but it has many tentacles stretching into feelings, backward from 1895, when it was written, and forward also. For you will notice that the line "Why mourn for Jesus?—Christ remains to us" accurately prophesies my "Idea of Christ in the Gospels," published more than fifty years later. 1895 had been the year of my first visit to Italy, in company with my friend Loeser, and it was on my return from there that I stopped at Arles, and other places in Southeastern France, before returning to America in a cattle-boat, for economy, from London to N.Y. in 16 days, without a touch of seasickness. I am not sure whether I speak of this voyage in any detail, or of the journey to Florence, Rome, Venice, and Milan, but they were all sentimentally important episodes for me at that time, when I was beginning to live my second, or rather, my third life after my "Change of Heart" in 1893, described in the first chapter of the third book of "Persons and Places." This was a reversion to solitude enriched by a great many absorbing scenes in the past and absorbing themes in the present and for the future. The sonnet in question has not been printed expressly because I think it would not be understood as yet: but it will appear in my "Posthumous Poems," which Cory will publish; and it occurs to me to say all this to you now, since you happen to have searched it out at the Congressional Library, to which I sent it (when asked for something) together with the portrait by Andreas Andersen, made one year later, when my College Life at the Harvard Yard was coming to an end. The next year 1896-7 I was at King's College; and when I returned to Harvard I lived in rooms in the town, like any outsider. All these things and others are pertinent, beginning with the Platonic Sonnets, to the various implications of that sonnet at Arles. I give you these hints, knowing that you are penetrating, and wishing that your penetration may go right. When do you expect to have your book done, soon or years hence? I should like to be able to read it before it is published. Yours sincerely   G. Santayana

The enclosure was an acknowledgment by Mr. David C. Mearns, Chief of the Manuscripts Division of the Library of Congress, to Santayana's request for release of the sonnet I had mentioned. On this letter, dated January 5, 1952, Santayana had written a postscript:

P.S. Feb. 25, '52

I had just sent off my letter about your sonnets on the VIA CRUCIS when this was returned to me—my second blunder in addressing letters to you. I send it again, hoping that this time it will reach you, as by chance it touches the same points as my last.

G.S.

My sonnet sequence, later renamed STATIONS OF THE CROSS, was originally meant to accompany pictures of each of the fourteen stations. Santayana's criticism, valuable in itself to me as criticism, also revealed something I was anxious to ferret out. What was his precise attitude toward the Faith in which he was born, and toward which he had always made such friendly gestures? Opinions differed. To some Santayana seemed genuinely Catholic, despite his protests to the contrary. To others he seemed the devil incarnate, though a census-taker would undoubtedly count him as one of the fold. His answer speaks for itself:

Via Santo Stefano Rotondo, 6,
Rome, 23rd Feb 1952

Dear Lind

I have read your VIA CRUCIS once, but carefully and with some reversion to confirm or correct the impressions received. There is an element—the spirit of the STABAT MATER—that is perfectly orthodox or Catholic but which I have never liked or shared. *All* devotion, for me in my boyhood, was festive, Good Friday just as festive as Easter or Christmas, and I have never felt the usual *distress* or *guiltiness* in the presence of Christ's martyrdom, or any other martyrdom. It may be a turn of mind—too mental—that made my countrymen like *Autos de Fe* and bullfights. But it is not pure cruelty or tendency to destroy whatever does not please me. Let others enjoy it if they can. So I say to the STABAT MATER, which I used to hear sung and knew by heart, words and music—but in Rossini's version! in the jolliest possible, lightest and most harmonious warblings. Was this simply bad taste? I think not.

Life is essentially an *élan vital*, as Bergson calls it; that is, it is a *passage* from one state to another. But art, or the immortalisation of Life, is a synthesis. You preserve and recompose each episode in the light of the others that accompany or replace it. You make a mosaic or rose window of history; existence does not carry you on, but becomes *truth* for you.

If you have my IDEA OF CHRIST at hand, look up what I say about the text, "My God, my God, why hast thou forsaken me?" I suggest that the reason is that Christ might forsake himself. The Jewish Messiah *had* to do that, or else to collapse morally. The *Christian* Christ outgrows his Palm Sunday illusion. David's kingdom was good for David: Jesus does not really want it for himself. His triumph is spiritual.

As I understand this it consists in the transcendence of Life into Truth or Art. I, or you for yourself, then fall out of the picture and the Via Crucis becomes a mosaic or a stained glass window. It does not make me *suffer now at all*. There is a great deal of crimson still in the picture, and a great deal of sorrow and mourning, but it is all a beautiful procession, no desire to banish it, or regret that it should have existed. But of course I don't want to live through it, or to have anyone else live through it again.

I am now not ready to pass any criticism on your sonnets. But I feel that you must not dedicate them to me. I have nothing of that harrowed or repentant spirit, or desire for more life in art; only more of life transfigured into truth, history, and art.— This is my first impression. The book with illustrations may change it.

Yours   G. Santayana

My answer to Santayana's letters contains so much that is necessary for understanding his later replies that I take the liberty of transcribing it in its entirety.

March 22, 1952

Dear Mr. Santayana:

Your last two letters arrived a day apart. A sudden turn in my fortunes made it impossible to reply to them before now. It so happens that the night school for veterans, which has afforded me so much leisure in the past six years, is drawing to a close. I have been searching for another night job. So far I have found nothing. Meanwhile, as insurance, I have taken a teaching position during the day with the city schools here, at the same time keeping the veterans' position, which continues on a part-time basis. As a result my leisure has vanished. This will continue till the last of May, when both jobs will lapse. In the fall, if I want it, the day work will be waiting for me. I shall be looking in the interim for a sinecure, such as time-keeper for owl buses or night-watchman in a tamale factory.

Your wishes concerning the VIA CRUCIS will be respected. It was kind of you to comment on it at all. Judging by your remarks and those of friends to whom I have shown it, it will cause endless controversy. Everyone, including yourself, seems completely taken in by its dramatic projection. This is not I speaking, but Catholicism. Strange as it may seem, I agree whole-heartedly with you about this lachrimose side of the cult. In one phase, Catholicism seems scarcely more than a vast guilt-manufacturing machine, for the better control of the faithful. Nevertheless—just as if the Eleusinian mysteries were still cele-brated in our midst—concerning all this I feel a poetic curiosity. It would be incorrect to claim that, unlike your Oliver, I sing what I do not feel. No. I feel what I do not necessarily identify with myself. The VIA CRUCIS is in fact part of a larger cycle of ritual verse long under way—almost a poetic VARIETIES OF RELI-GIOUS EXPERIENCE—not confined to "slumming." (I was re-ferring here to Santayana's objection to William James' book, as religious slumming.) In this cycle I explore everything, from Nirvana among Buddhists to fornication among Quakers. But why all this? you may ask—particularly when I do not identify myself with it.

This brings me to your writings. The moral world, you have said, has been circumnavigated a thousand times. This is the realm of religion. I think it no accident that church bells ring. They echo the white-hot iron of desire clanging on the anvil of necessity. Whether the heart's desire be a consummation, an accident, a scandal or a fraud in the physical universe, I think some religion has already developed the attitudes and symbols appropriate to the predicament. If we are to be moral we must know this. In a word, the overwhelming and universal sense of most religions that revelation is "complete" simply reflects the heart's sense that it knows what it wants and how it would feel—given a particular physical environment. But this latter world was circumnavigated only in 1519, and then only terrestrially. It is to the *continuous* revelation of science that the heart of modern man must answer. But the answer lies dormant under ashes of religion and myth. Northrop has said "The more the contemporary institutions and practices conform to the original aesthetic intuition of the ancient and primitive past, the better; . . . the more they conform (in their theoretic aspect) to the most technical scientific conceptions of the present the better." (MEETING OF EAST AND WEST, page 458) Thus, at any given moment in the history of science, the spiritual insights of some historical religion may still be valid. It is idle to invent all this symbolism anew. What is not idle is to show that beneath even the most archaic symbols of the heart's desire the heart still beats—forever young. And the heart, I presume, is the poet's realm. It is legitimate, then, if somewhat confusing, to feel an alien cult. The cult is an armature for portraying the eternal dilemma of incarnate spirit. Only in the latter sense do I identify myself with it at all, as you do likewise if I am not mistaken.

You ask when my book on you will be finished. I can only

reply that the book on Murger, where I had to do a lot of translating, took two years. So soon as any chapter of it is in respectable form, I shall send you the typescript.

On one point I feel you can give me valuable assistance. I have read VERA. Also, in our conversations last year, you agreed that Jim Darnley was a mask for Russell—deliberately deformed, I am sure. The other night, quite in the manner of Sherlock Holmes, I sat smoking my pipe when it suddenly occurred to me that Russell must have killed somebody! The death of Vera in the novel is put down as suicide. The death of the mate on the yacht is put down to an over-dose of sleeping tablets, perhaps administered by Lord Jim. At this late date, if there is any truth in my conjectures, I see no harm in stating it. If there is none, you can easily set me right. Naturally, without further confirmation, I should never put forward such a theory on the basis of the documentation alone. The evidence is too thin. But here, if my intuition is correct, you can keep me on the right track. It would not be the first skeleton to be found in a lordly family. And, what is more to the point, it would not bother you, as it doesn't bother me, hearing it rattle.

With best regards and kindly memories of just one year ago,
                                                         Bruno

Santayana, as the letter below demonstrates, took my little difficulties more seriously than I did myself. I was not worried about a job, only about one which would leave me leisure to write. The Veterans' Training Program had been in this respect a bonanza.

                                    Via Santo Stefano Rotondo, 6,
                                    Rome, March 27, 1952

Dear Lind

I am surprised and very sorry to hear that you are having difficulties as to your occupations. My surmise was that you were a teacher in a High School, like the Boston Latin School, which is responsible for my free but superficial education, and which was a most regular and ancient establishment. These night schools for veterans coming to an end and temporary employment in town schools seem insecure and unsatisfactory. I hope you will find something that may leave you time for your literary projects.

That your VIA CRUCIS is a part of a sort of poetic anthology of religious passions changes my impression of those sonnets and their morbid sensibility. As I said in my letter this is orthodox Catholic sentiment, but not dominant in Christian devotion as a whole. Of the 15 mysteries of the Rosary only five a(re) "dolorous," the others being either "joyful" or "glorious." But female piety is often accentuated by bereavements. I shall be greatly interested in seeing the whole collection.

It is true that, especially in "THE IDEA OF CHRIST" (I) have attempted just such an interpretation of one phase of religious feeling, without pretending to believe in the legend that supplies the particular instance described. But I have distinguished what I sincerely believe to be the spiritual insight of a man living— as Aristotle recommends (without having practised it) as much as possible in the eternal—That is not sentimental nor even humanitarian, but purely intellectual. As a man, however, is much besides intellect, the rest of his nature has to be somewhat objectified and defeated in assuming the divine view of it all.

As to the character, and especially the conversation, of the *young* Russell, being attributed by me to Lord Jim, that is very true, and was recognised by the latter's wife, Elizabeth, author of "VERA," who however did not reproduce it in her book. What she reproduced was only his domestic fussiness and exactions—from which I never suffered, on the contrary, living with him, even at close quarters, as in his yacht, was (as he put it himself) the most "lotus-eating" life possible. As to my Lord Jim's temptation to make troublesome persons disappear, Russell never had it. He had always been in command, and had always believed he had a right to mastery over wives and servants. But this he felt to be *virtuous* severity, as is perhaps not clear enough in "VERA." Lady R. was too exasperated to be fair on this point.

Yours sincerely   G Santayana

P.S. My question as to when your book about me would be published was prompted only by the sense that I should not live to see it. I feel better now and think I may live a while longer.

On June 8, 1952, I wrote Santayana as follows:

"The postscript to your last letter, saying that your health was mending, was good news indeed. I hope that the Roman spring has been kind to you, that you are making progress in your revision of THE LIFE OF REASON, and that you will forgive this long delay in communicating with you . . . I hope to resume work on your book henceforth. Below you will find various excerpts from my notes which may or may not elicit your comment."

Of the excerpts mentioned, Santayana commented specifically on but two—itself a feat, in view of the catastrophe he reports in his next letter. My notes concerning which he was able to make remarks ran as follows:

"A certain lack of manual dexterity in his youth may have led Santayana to overemphasize the gap between action and reflection. A more athletic youth might have led to less marked a distinction."

"In SOLILOQUIES IN ENGLAND Santayana describes sane philosophy as 'a commentary, not a dream.' Elsewhere he suggests that philosophy itself is poetry, a dream—only more or less modulated by contact with 'reality.' 'Normal madness' is loosely corrected by Punishment and Agreement. Such a chastened madness, however, is no longer mad; and Santayana tends, in REALMS OF BEING, to agree with Lin Yutang in thinking that 'Truly great ritualism shares the principles of distinction with the universe.' "

Via Santo Stefano Rotondo, 6,
Rome. June 14, 1952

Dear Lind,

I may repeat in beginning this letter what I seem to have said at the end of my last, but not by announcing a *continuous* convalescence. One June 4th I had an accident very nearly fatal. I fell backwards going down the (artificial) marble stairs at the Spanish Consulate, and struck the edges of the steps with the back of my head and with my side. I saw it happen, as I was going down cautiously with one hand grasping the rail; but when I tried to get up, I lost consciousness. On coming to, I found myself being carried into my taxi by a lot of men: four got inside with me, and a fifth next the chauffeur in front. When the doctor examined me, he said no bones were broken, but only a few abrasions, only one (on the head) bleeding. He put patches on these and gave me some anaesthetic which dulled all pain. The worst, they said later, had been the severe shock.

The consulate people (the one that held me was, I think, the vice-consul) were very attentive and told the Sisters that they were in charge and would pay for everything. I am in much better odour in Spain now than ever in my life before.

This is the accident: the rest has been only warding off fever by repeated injections—.

Another day I will answer your "notes" in detail. They are all well grounded, only that other considerations, in some cases, seem to me more crucial. My athletic incompetence, and generally my "psyche" compared with my speculative leanings, does not so much produce over-emphasis on spiritual things as over-valuing the perfection of (Greek) physical virtues. My denial of an intrinsic moral dignity or power in essences contrasts with Bertrand Russell's original worship of mathematics as "true." They are only *correct*, but, like music, have marvellous harmonious complexity which delights the intellect as music does the spirit. Truth proper does not come in, because mathematics and music reveal nothing except themselves. But that is no reason for poopooing them, as Russell now does essences. They are the

intrinsic exercises and joys of mind. But a perfect bodiless mind
would not be a perfect man; only an insipid angel.

Seeing that you are working on my biography, I will send
you shortly a very sympathetic "poem" about me as an undergraduate at Harvard by a man I never knew, Eugene Shippen of
the class of 1887.

Yours sincerely

G Santayana

Late in June, the promised poem arrived, with the commentary below.

Via Santo Stefano Rotondo, 6,

Rome. June 26, 1952

Dear Lind

I have delayed sending you the blank verse of my eulogist
Shippen because Miss Tindall, whom I meant to copy it, has
been having her precious holiday in England. But meantime
I have reread the eulogy and think it is not worth quoting in
any history or criticism about me, because he misrepresents
too many points in my sentiments and motives. He did not
know me personally, and let his imagination and prejudices
loose. Nevertheless I send you the "Poem" and his letter that
came with it, to show you what a nineteenth century American
of the expatriate type could think of me. You may keep the
document or throw it away: I do not care that it should be
taken seriously. There would be more nonsense than truth in
doing so. What chiefly pleased me at first was that he should
have taken me for an exiled patrician when I was a penniless
waif and my American friends, also the English, my social
models. It was really true that I was morally independent, until
I found my masters in the ancients.

Yours sincerely

G Santayana

My next letter to Santayana has tragic over-tones, because the sage's days, after his accident, were numbered. Here are excerpts from my rather flipppant letter:

"Were you trying to end your days on Spanish soil, even in Rome? Thank heaven you emerged with just a few bumps and bruises! Let us hope this finds you restored to health and resolved not to fall again . . . Herewith you are receiving the first chapter of the book, disguised as a preface, itself disguised as a warning (so that somebody will read it!)"

The above was written on July 8, 1952. Santayana must have set about reading my Preface immediately. Very shortly he returned it, annotated, and accompanied by his last note to me. The handwriting was shakier than usual, and, unlike all the other letters was written in pencil.

One comment on our "disagreement" requires clarification. I had ended my Preface as follows:

"A final word. It is hard, at least for me, to write about Santayana without enthusiasm . . . At the same time, let the reader take warning: this book is not an apology for his system; it does not purport to belong to his 'school,' if any. The fact is, I find myself in sharp disagreement with him on a number of points, as will appear in the following pages. In particular, I take issue with him in the sphere of aesthetics, where I feel relatively competent."

Santayana's reply dealt, among other things, with this paragraph.

July 18, 1952

Dear Lind

I have read this twice and find it splendid. My eyes are getting weak and uncertain, so that both reading and writing are difficult. In my first reading I thought perhaps you repeated your classification too much, and that "Intellectuals" was vague. But I felt this less on the second reading; also missed altogether a quotation that I meant to ask you to leave out, although I did not understand it. This makes me think that the difference of "aesthetic" views between us is only a difference in taste in some particulars; for my aesthetic theory or criterion of excellence is a part of my *ethics*, and not dogmatic. Each real artist has a message of his own. No one else is obliged to share it nor (except as a part of politics or ethics) even to exclude it from his sympathy.

What occurred to me (*sic*) that the most radical way of describing my ethics is to say that its principle is not Duty but Virtue. It is only when a particular duty is an exercise of *Natural virtue* that it can be binding morally.

G.S.

Shortly after Santayana's fall on the steps of the Spanish consulate, I had noticed that the Spanish Royal Academy had awarded a decoration to the British historian, Arnold Toynbee. Here was an English man of letters, and an Anglican, being honored by Spain while one of her own sons, Santayana, had nearly perished on Spanish soil, without receiving notice from his countrymen. I was not inclined to cast aspersions on Toynbee's decoration: it was richly deserved, but Santayana deserved it also. The homage did suggest that religious differences no longer counted in such cultural matters. Together with Mr. Leonidas Gonzalez, editor of LA PRENSA in San Antonio, and Mr. Henry Gonzalez, editor of the ENGLISH-SPANISH REVIEW, I wrote a letter to the Spanish ambassador in Washington, calling attention to Santayana's plight. Señor Lequerica replied shortly that he was quite aware of Santayana's importance and that the matter had been referred to Madrid.

Meanwhile, Mr. Cory, Santayana's secretary, was called back from England because of Santayana's grave condition after his fall. I have the following account from Mr. Cory himself:

"A few days later he developed pneumonia and the Sisters telephoned me in England saying that they expected he would die. I at once flew down to Rome on a Comet and found him in a very bad state. But with the help of penicillin he made an astonishing recovery, and two weeks later I was able to return to England and he was up in his room and working on a translation into English of a poem by Lorenzo de Medici entitled *Ambra* . . . Then sometime in August his eyesight began to fail rapidly (he had cataracts) and he could hardly read or write anything. When I got back to Rome on September 10 I found him in very poor shape. His color was yellow and he could hardly hold any food at all. His doctor then informed me that he had cancer of the stomach and could not possibly live much longer. The last two weeks of his life he suffered considerably and had to have injections of morphia. But he resolutely refused to see any priest and the question of extreme unction was not even raised . . . No doubt you have read in the newspapers of his burial in the *Tomba degli Spagnuoli* here in the Verano Catholic Cemetery in Rome, so there is no need at the moment for me to enlarge upon that simple but moving event."

As obituaries began to appear in various journals, I was struck by one article, handed me by Mr. Leonidas Gonzales, which had appeared in the Spanish paper, *ABC*, of October 2, 1952. Had our intervention on the sage's behalf borne fruit? I wrote Mr. Cory:

"It so happens that shortly after Mr. Santayana's fall I wrote the Spanish Embassy suggesting that some homage from Spain would be appropriate, particularly if awarded during his life-time . . . Now . . . I find a report of an interview handed by you, typed, to the Spanish correspondent in Rome, Sr. Julian Cortes Cavanillas, touching upon this matter—or so it seems. The final question was: 'Would you be pleased by some homage from Spain?' (I'm translating from the Spanish.) The rest of the interview seemed a preliminary survey of Mr. Santayana's patriotic sentiments and his relative esteem of Catholicism. I am curious whether all this was spontaneous or the outcome of orders from Madrid."

As to "orders from Madrid," Mr. Cory was non-committal, but, alas! our intervention had come too late. The

answers to the correspondent's questions were perhaps indica-
tive of Santayana's sentiments; the words, however, were Cory's.
He replied:
"The interview I had with the Spanish correspondent in
Rome occurred about four days before the Master's death.
He was in a semi-coma and obviously unable to answer for
himself. So I took it upon myself to answer a set of fixed
questions that were fired at me."

Whether Santayana will yet be honored by his native land,
which by his writings he did so much to honor, remains to
be seen.

As for myself, when news came over the radio that Santayana had died, my telephone began ringing. Next day, to
escape further calls from solicitous friends, I got into my car
and drove to the top of a hill which houses Trinity University
and overlooks all San Antonio. It was a hot September noon.
Roundabout, crickets were chirping. In the shimmering sunshine, amidst cactus and mesquite, I was aware of a certain
desolation which hangs over both Texas and Spain—a desert
vastness. Before me I saw:

"Black in the noon the broad estates of Death."

My heart
was very full.

I wondered then whether anyone in Spain or America or
the whole wide world would ever understand Santayana, or do
him proper homage. A week later I wrote him my last letter.
The "book" referred to there is of course not this book but
BOHEMIAN OF THE INFINITE.

October 1, 1952
Dear, honored friend:
It is hard for me to stop writing to you, though you reside
no longer at San Stefano Rotondo, 6, in the Eternal City, but
rather at an address unknown in a Heavenly City—which may
or may not exist.
Less than a week ago I was composing in my mind the

usual letter: "Enclosed you will find some chapters of your book. If you have the strength and feel the inclination you may wish to comment. Here, also, are a few additional questions . . ." And presently—but now no more—I expected to receive your prompt reply in the familiar script and with the usual remarks: so cheerful, so apt, so witty—and so utterly humble. Now you have joined my other genial Bohemians, of whom I had hoped at least one—yourself—would be among the living.

Yet we had both known—had we not?—that it would be a race against Time. Time, in fact, has been gracious to us. Not only were we able to discuss this book together in Rome, but thereafter, in lengthy correspondence, we dealt with special questions. Finally, you were able to read the Preface and return it, annotated, with an appreciative word.

When, however, you reported in June that you had fallen on the "(artificial) marble" steps of the Spanish Consulate, I became anxious. I even quipped: "Are you unconsciously trying to end your days on Spanish soil?" What a bitter jest! Now I find I must go the rest of this way alone, lacking your kindly hand upon my shoulder. And no longer, I realize sadly, need there be any race against Time.

Would this book have pleased you, had you seen it to the end? I can only wish that it might. I can only hope that in its present form it may not deviate too much from the thing it might have been, written throughout with your guidance.

You may remember that when I was in Madrid a landslide prevented me from visiting your ancestral home in Avila. Somehow I felt this obstacle was only temporary. Eventually I shall visit Avila. So with this more serious obstacle: it is an accident, I think, but nothing more.

If, then, I venture to hope that this volume may not prove an unworthy memorial, I do so keenly conscious of its faults, but also despite them. Of you, of the suffering, mortal being you lately were—of the flesh in which spirit is necessarily trapped—I have written a great deal: yet over this, surely, some few tears must be shed. Time is fatally cruel to all flesh. Of your spirit, dwelling by preference in Essence and the Eternal, I have perhaps written less than I ought: yet toward spirit nothing but joy can be felt. Time cannot touch it: its mansions are set in another, timeless dimension.

Besides, spirit and flesh were in you so joined that neither strutted as enemy of the other: the two remained friends. *Media morte in vita sumus*: in you the ancient maxim was reversed. And in the midst of death and all perishable things we too can live if—like you—we live in worship of the Eternal. Spirit—"Bohemian of the Infinite"—thus needs no memorial. It intermits. It is never lost.

Friendship also, if addressed to things of the spirit, partakes of the Eternal. I shall not express the hope, therefore, in closing this my last letter to you, dear friend, that we may meet again. Friends of the spirit are never parted.

Bruno

INDEX

INDEX